MW00948084

Tempting the Throne Room

Surviving Pakistan's Deadliest Climbing Season 2013

By: John Quillen

Copyright 2013 John Quillen
Edited by Eric Graves
Formatted by Polgarus Studio

CONTENTS

ACKNOWLEDGEMENTS

This book would not have been possible without the assistance of my expedition team and their recollections of events. I specifically like to thank Scott Powrie, Ron Hoglin and Ramin Shojaei for taking the time to ensure that the record included multiple corroborative sources. It is the intent of the author to provide a factual timeline of events but there is always the potential for mistakes or omissions for which I apologize in advance.

I also appreciate the assistance and support of Adventure Tours Pakistan and specifically NaikNam Karim, Ashraf Aman and Zoltan for their tireless efforts throughout the ordeal.

There were many angels who guided us through dark times and none less important than Joanna Henning who networked and kept communications flowing for friends and family and provided unlimited emotional support. Her initial editorial contributions helped shape the vision of this work. She was roped up to all of us from beginning to well beyond return.

I wish to thank Raheel Adnan, climbing journalist, who kept his finger on the pulse of all things Karakoram.

And many thanks to my editor, Eric Graves for his tireless efforts assimilating this manuscript. A friend is someone who tells you what you need to hear, an editor tells you what you have to hear. I am fortunate to call him both.

Dr. Dan Walters provided extensive medical and photographic support and my Denali team was there in spirit.

Angie Dobbs created the cover art.

And to my climbing partner, Brian Moran. He's a good one to have in your foxhole.

And to Shelby, for praying us back to safety and health.

I dedicate this book to Mom and Dad for devoting a lifetime to keeping our base camp avalanche and rock fall free through storms that buried the tents of other families.

IN MEMORY OF AIDIN BOZORGI, POUYA KEYVAN AND MOJTABA JARAHI

Iran and the climbing world never knew better ambassadors.

For he wounds, but he also binds up;
he injures, but his hands also heal.
19 From six calamities he will rescue you;
in seven no harm will touch you.
20 In famine he will deliver you from death,
and in battle from the stroke of the sword.
21 You will be protected from the lash of the tongue,
and need not fear when destruction comes.
22 You will laugh at destruction and famine,
and need not fear the wild animals.
23 For you will have a covenant with the stones of the field,
and the wild animals will be at peace with you.
24 You will know that your tent is secure;
you will take stock of your property and find nothing missing

Job 5: 18-24

PROLOGUE

There is no doubt that the Karakoram seems at times a God-forsaken place. Every natural object appears designed to snatch breath and life from human beings. From the boulders at Urdukas to the avalanching slopes of K2 and Gasherbrum, the rocky snowfields on these high mountains don't deserve respect, they command it. Be it threading a needle through the Labyrinthine icefalls to teetering on a bamboo bridge keeping guard over K3's ramparts, these Himalayan giants exact equal measures of fear and awe.

When you're on the mountain after a month and things aren't going so well, fantasies of civilization roll in like storm clouds over your judgment. The gravitational pull of basecamp creates a phenomena I dubbed "pizza eyes". Seen it too many times. You get focused on down climbing to an oasis of perceived luxury where meals are served and water doesn't need melting from snow. It's a great irony that, while on the mountain, you fantasize of these things then, strangely when back in the soup of humanity, despite all the hardship and forbearance, would gladly drop every money making task, abandon friends and family to trade that desk and buffet of existence for those boulders, snow and fixed rope. It is a mountaineer's disease that pulls us back to these places because, for whatever reason, it feels like where we are supposed to be. I don't say home because it is a seasonal migration. Perhaps it is where we spawn but I'm not sure what offspring is birthed.

2013 was the deadliest year ever seen in the Karakoram. On Broad Peak alone, 7 deaths represent 20.6% of all fatalities on the mountain since it was first climbed in 1957 by a group including Kurt Diemberger via the route that we used and is considered standard today. The deaths in 2013 moved Broad Peak above Shishapangma to make it the 8th deadliest of the

8000 meter mountains of the earth, now twice as deadly as Everest, Lhotse, Gasherbrum 2 and Cho Oyu combined.

In March of this year a group of Poles made the first successful winter attempt of the mountain but at a great price. Two alpinists perished on the descent, Tomasz Kowalski and Maciej Berbeka's bodies were found during our expedition by a group comprised of professional mountaineers, one of whom was Jecek Berbeka, brother of Maciej. The funeral dirge began as we leap frogged up and down the glacier with them from Skardu to basecamp. Little did I realize the tragedy that would carry us out of this place and the smell of death that was to linger long after our return to civilization.

Paiyu campsite is 85 miles as the crow flies from Nanga Parbat, the 9th highest mountain in the world. It lies along a 100 plus mile trail that has been dubbed, "the greatest museum of shapes and forms" on earth. This is where our team was spending a rest day on June 22, 2013 when Taliban terrorists, disguised as local police, stormed Nanga Parbat basecamp and brutally murdered 11 mountain climbers of varying nationalities. One of them was an American.

Straddling the dusty Indus River bank we caught wind of the tragedy via satellite phone text message from team member Scott Powrie's wife, Leigh, in Malaysia. We were now three days into our seven day trek to the base camp of Broad Peak where we planned to live for two months while making an attempt of that mountain. Plans for other attacks in our region were a growing concern, but no one dared breathe word of this fear the next morning as we slouched up towards the Baltoro glacier in the blazing sun. Little did we realize the price that was to be paid for tempting the throne room of the mountain gods.

Below is my account of our ill-fated and tragic foray into the Karakoram Range to climb this remote peak in the shadow of K2. Broad Peak is also known as K3.

KARAKORAM DREAMS;

Rawalpinidi, Pakistan June 8, 2013

I'm standing in a hot, airless room with dozens of other foreigners. None are from my part of the world. Fans sit high in the windows allowing the sun's first rays but they aren't doing much good for the rising heat. A motionless carousel is the object of everyone's attention and the contents we hope to find soon circling upon it. There are muted announcements high in the background in a strange language I will come to easily identify in upcoming weeks as Urdu. Every now and then I detect some interspersed English phrase.

Many months of planning, training and logistical preparation culminate in this arrival in Islamabad on June 10, 2013. My girlfriend Joanna accompanied me from Knoxville to New York in order to catch flights to Kuwait then eventually Islamabad. We rented a car for the drive to JFK in order to transport the massive amount of luggage required for this expedition. I couldn't risk mixing a domestic and foreign flight should my bags not make any leg so we turned it into a small, mini vacation. Plus, Joanna had friends in the city, and I was appreciative of her company and assistance. We had begun dating about three months prior to this expedition and the climbing life was definitely a mystery to her. We swung round the international terminal and hastily said goodbye as I picked up two out of three monstrous duffels while scouting for a cart. I was not slated to return for two months.

Departing New York on Kuwait Airlines, I stop for a transit in London where I am harassed mercilessly and subjected to another, seemingly superfluous security checkpoint. Half a day later I reach Kuwait City surrounded by a gallery of the most interesting and uniquely adorned people on the planet. It is like being at the bar in the Star Wars movie surrounded by many colorful keffiyahs, turbans, robes and other headgear. I was definitely under dressed. So begins my immersion into this Islamic world. I had been to Arab lands before, but not for this length of time.

A four-hour flight was all that separated me from Pakistan; I soon plunge headlong into the heat of this nation's capital. Moving seamlessly through customs I am deposited at this baggage claim in the inner sanctum of the capital's flagship airport. I think of all the times I have entered a foreign land not knowing what to expect from its people and institutions on similar journeys chasing mountains. The baggage area is old and hot and it could as easily be 1953 were anyone to photograph the scene. The rickety carousel begins vomiting various bags and boxes. Within a few minutes I spy two of my three bags, meticulously weighing in at 50 lbs. apiece. The big black one never emerges from the bowels of the carousel after everyone has departed, and as if on cue, the fans and carousel fall silent.

Brownouts are a common malady in Pakistan, I soon learn. One of the bugs this nascent nation has yet to correct is variable power availability. I quickly become accustomed to the erratic nature of electricity in hotel rooms and showers. But at this moment, what really matters is that my big bag is missing … It portends subsequent mishandlings.

The Pakistanis give me documents in lieu of the big bag, but they are in Urdu, the unofficial language of the country. Ironically, English is the official language but you would never know it as a result of speaking with anyone. Forty five minutes of this and it is time for me to enter the fray amassing beyond the security gates. Imagine a sea of men clamoring for your attention as you negotiate with super heavy luggage hoping all the while that nothing goes missing from either bag or backpack hanging off your shoulder. I spot a short man holding a sign from Adventure Tours Pakistan, our ground agent. His gracious smile and lack of English matter little as he whisks me to the requisite terminal where a waiting van is gassed and porters load my gear. Having contacts on the ground in alien turf is such tremendous relief. I board the bus and peer from the safety of a window at the hundreds of human beings, all men and all dressed alike.

My introduction to Pakistani traffic occurs at six a.m. local time. The hot dust of Rawalpindi (*Islamabad is actually a split city, the airport is really in "Pindi"*) and the early hour do nothing to lessen the zoo of motorcycles and overloaded vehicles with men hanging off every open bumper and door handle. I see six people, a complete family, on one, single cylinder motorcycle.

Figure 1: Scenes like this were common
Photo Brian Moran

We drive for 30 minutes to the Envoy Continental Hotel, passing several security checkpoints. I offload and am smacked by heat of the early morning at a hotel in the "Blue Zone". It is reminiscent of Baghdad or some other bombed out war area. I consider the designation in light of terrorist involvement. Living in Pakistan for two months, such notions are unavoidable. It is Pakistan, for goodness sake. Protestations of friends, family and even acquaintances always involved Talibanic innuendo and rightfully so. My standard defense was straight from the adventure tourism playbook. No terrorist acts had been perpetuated upon any climber at any time in the region. Climbing is so remote and takes place in such a peaceful area that the statistics simply didn't justify the fears. With that, I successfully disarmed my loved ones and attempted to minimize their understandable fears.

At the Envoy hotel in the Blue Zone, a guard holds the door, AK 47 slung casually over his shoulder. I am seated in the lobby and greeted by Mr. Ashraf Aman. Ashraf, now in his late 60s, is the first Pakistani to summit the world's second highest and arguably most dangerous peak, K2 in 1977. He is a real life, Pakistani national hero. Ashraf is the owner of Adventure Tours Pakistan (ATP). ATP is our ground agent that essentially handles our adventure from start to finish. We had originally contracted through Field Touring Alpine who, in turn, subcontracts with ATP for services. Ashraf is a colorful man who takes his company and clients quite seriously.

Staff at the Envoy greet me with a Coke, and I spend an hour chatting in the lobby with Ashraf. (*I should inject here that air conditioning is optional in most all of Pakistan.*) This particular day was becoming one of the warmest on record; we would see 110 degrees by noon. The Coke is a delight, however and I head back toward the lobby counter to grab another sip of the glass's cool contents but Ashraf picks it up and takes a sip. Deleterious implications notwithstanding, I should have abandoned all hope of hygiene entirely at this point. My greatest fear for this expedition wasn't avalanches or crevasses. Given my history of gastrointestinal susceptibility to any foreign microbe and virus, my friend Dave McGhee, upon hearing of my plans for Pakistan pronounced, *"Well, you haven't puked on that country yet."*

I was anxious to retreat to my room and relax for a few minutes. It was still quite early, and the bag/travel ordeal was prescient. Brian and the remainder of our climbing team would be arriving soon. Our leader, Ron Hoglin, is already around somewhere. After washing up and changing clothes, I return to the lobby where Brian, Scott Powrie (*another expedition member*) and Ron have now assembled on the Persian couches in the hot lobby. Ron and Brian somehow hooked up in Dubai. You get pretty good at spotting fellow climbers. I'll bet my buddy Brian had him pegged immediately. Scott is obviously in good shape and excited about his first 8000 meter attempt. I hadn't seen Brian in over half a year and he displays that award winning smile as he arises in greeting.

Ron Hoglin manages to extricate himself from the sticky couch to shake hands with me as I drop back into the hot lobby after an hour respite in my tiny room on the third floor. His accent is decidedly North American, eh? With Nordic features and slim build this was to be his first try leading an expedition after the original leader, Chris Szymiec, backed out. Looking at him you would never guess that Ron's climbing resume included two summits of Everest from the North and South, a summit of Lhotse and an attempt on K2 wherein he reached camp 4. He also completed multiple solo ascents of North America's highest peak, Denali. Scott Powrey is a Californian now living in Malaysia. He is a welder/engineer type with a helicopter pilot's license. Between he and Brian, our team was covered on the pilot front (*Brian flies for Delta Airlines*) we should have any potential evacuation plan nailed, I thought.

Ron introduces us to a guy joining him on the couch, Tunc Findic. I knew of Tunc from his well-documented accomplishments on the high peaks in varying mountaineering journals. Ron and Tunc had climbed together on K2 in 2009 and he would spend some days here in Islamabad before departing for Nanga Parbat. I thought about that mountain and its reputation for danger but at well over 6 feet 5 and as experienced as they come, I was certain he had the good sense to handle it. Tunc is a constant figure the few days we spend in this capital city. He was a genuinely nice guy and Turkey's most prominent alpinist.

It is decided that we should proceed to exchange money for our two months in country. Darting across the dusty and ever warming streets of Islamabad, Brian is diverted to gain an extension on his visa. If I have any gift it is an ability to blend easily into dark skinned cultures. With white skin and red hair, Brian gathers the errant glances from Pakistani men assembled on the streets that I fortunately seem to avoid. His American-ness is undeniable. Add Ron's Vancouver accent and we were the focus of all things Islamabad on this scalding June morning.

We are soon dodging traffic and in search of a place to offload dollars for rupees. If anyone knows how to navigate foreign cultures, it is Brian. His work and travels have taken him across the globe and there is no situation or confrontation for which he does not readily have an answer. There was the time in Lima when we were hauling our mountain of gear to a mountain unknown. Sticking from the hulking mound were bamboo wands that we intended to employ for route finding high in the Andes. Peruvian security was more than a little interested in these homemade contrivances and began fondling them skeptically. Before a nosy guard could even open his mouth, Brian grabbed the duffel from which the sticks were protruding, snatched them from the official and said, *"They are agricultural markers."* Whatever that meant, it had a desired effect and we proceeded undeterred into the country.

Ashraf was to shepherd him through this visa extension process. I was lucky enough to have received 60 days permission on my initial application. This is apparently another common problem with Pakistan. Climbers routinely have to seek extensions beyond the 30-day period, despite the well- known fact that all the eight thousand meter peaks take a minimum of two months in country. It is just another example of an inefficient bureaucratic process that plagues the people and visitors of this Republic. Another full day would pass before Brian returns to the Envoy Hotel with documents in hand. His introduction to Pakistan is through the window of hot taxis and stops at multiple government offices.

Figure 2: Left to right: the author, Brian Moran, Ron Hoglin and Scott Powrie
Photo Scott Powrie

Fast forward two days. Brian has his visa extension (*it involved the mayor of Pakistan*), I have returned to the airport and retrieved my errant luggage and we are all preparing for the 30-hour bus ride to Skardu, our disembarkation point for the jeep ride to Askole. From Askole we would begin a 100 mile walk to the Baltoro Glacier. An extra day in Islamabad to deal with the aforementioned issues means exposure to the heat of an unbearably dusty desert aridity. It also includes a tour of the city and mosques, compliments of ATP that my partner misses. Growing along the side of the hills are fields of marijuana with small button buds protruding from the stalky weed. I finger the plant to see if it is similar to my memories of the substance. Same thing, different place. This is deemed worthy of several pictures especially since the locals and monkeys, of all things, pass undeterred along the hill that houses a city park and overlook.

Next we are taken to the Faisal Mosque. For seven years this was the largest mosque in the world until being overtaken by additions to similar structures in Saudi Arabia, who financed the construction of this massive edifice. It is a matter of great pride for our Pakistani tour guide. The only female member of our expedition, Gangaama Badamgarav, draws the stares that would have been reserved for Brian as she weaves through the carpeted prayer rugs in shorts with a video camera. "*Ganga*" is the first Mongolian woman to summit Mt. Everest.

From left to right: John, Ron, Afshin, Aidin, Pouya, Ganga, Mojtaba (Photo: Scott Powrie)

The Karakoram Highway to Hell
Figure 3: Wreckage highlights danger of KKH
Photo Brian Moran

If we were ever going to make it to Broad Peak and begin our 100 plus mile one way walk through some of the harshest landscape on earth, there was something even more dreadful with which we first had to contend. No crevasse, avalanche or altitudinal fear held me more captive than the prospect of enduring this road, again. Not to mention the potential exposure to an act of terrorism for which this area was developing a solid reputation. My anxiety was experienced based, having swallowed a good taste of it from the Chinese side two years prior on an expedition to Muztagh Ata. During that trip we spent two days negotiating hairpin turns with a maniacal driver. The Karakoram Highway was a joint project between the countries of Pakistan and China and was touted as an engineering breakthrough and possible economic conduit between two depressed regions. There are sections of this, largely dirt, road that drop almost a thousand feet to the Indus River. Weekly reports of deaths led to a US television series highlighting the perils of traveling this path carved from the sides of mountains. It is generally considered the most dangerous road on earth.

5:30 a.m., June 12,

Figure 4: Scott photographs Afshin explaining something to Aidin as Mojtaba looks on.
Photo Scott Powrie

Gear is crammed into a small bus and each of us are jockeying for the most advantageous seats. We are finally departing Islamabad for Skardu. The morning is rainy and cools the dusty street as we drag ourselves and luggage onto the cramped vehicle. I am now suffering full on from a stomach bug that manifest in varying, unmentionable ways, none of which are conducive to long bus journeys on the most dangerous road on the planet. Joining us are five members of an Iranian team that will be sharing our climbing permit. Three are 20 something men who laugh and giggle while I keep near the window, just in case. These kids are exceptionally affable, engaging and have limited English skills. It is Aidin Bozorgi's second try on Broad Peak, and their goal is to put up a new route from camp 3. I laud their ambition and drive. Pouya Keyvan and Aidin are constantly smiling and Aidin seems to have a knack for getting the giggle out of Pouya. Mojtaba Jarahi is a little more serious but very respectful. We would grow to become very close as the weeks pass. I immediately realize that all three have the same model of obscure climbing boots as myself. *(It confers that they did thorough research and exercise extreme thrift.)* The other two Iranians are older and somewhat less hyperactive.

During the first day of winding roads we pass through Abbottabad, the town where Osama Bin Laden was killed by U.S Navy Seals. I realize this as we are gazed up through the bus windows like creatures in a circus tent by men who all resembled aforementioned dead terrorist.

"Pretty easy for him to blend into this environment," I remark as our carriage slings my head against the window again.

We round a corner and stop near a roadside fruit stand. I hope to snag some more melon or mango to settle my disquieted stomach. Instead, a dark skinned, stern faced man in a wool uniform and sawed off machine gun boards. Staring each of us down intently he reaches his hand out to me and I pause for an awkward two seconds not knowing what to do. Working his way down the aisle he shakes everyone's hand before settling in a seat next to the window. Fortunately, he is not a terrorist but Pakistani policeman who accompanies our troupe for a couple of hours from one checkpoint to the next. No explanations were offered and none requested. We are in Taliban territory here. As we approach the blockaded areas, other uniformed police board the bus and shake each of our hands. I can only surmise that they either think us quite brave or wish to be the last human to press our flesh.

After offloading this police guy and stopping for lunch (*I was now as miserable as a human could be as a result of the stomach issue and the only thing appealing about lunch was the notion of stopping this death machine for an hour*), we press on to experience the full bore of the Karakoram Highway. My former experience didn't hold a candle to this roller coaster. In 2011 we were treated to the Chinese side of this carnival ride on our way to climb Muztagh Ata in the Chinese Pamirs. I never imagined anything approaching the terror of that experience but quickly wished for a trade. This is the most dangerous road on the planet, for real. Hairpin turns, absent shoulders, rockslides and bad driving claim many, many lives along this two-day ordeal. The vertical banks of sand and boulders are littered with fresh vehicles that have rolled hundreds of feet. Not to mention my stomach condition that is worsening. And it never fails that I get saddled with some driver who has something to prove. You would think that a normal reaction to these driving conditions would be to modify your speed. Oh no, not with this idiot. He seems to take it as a challenge that he should bear these curves with increasing speed. There are times when he takes corners so fast the bus tilts towards the river and I am on that side. Approaching vehicles are nearly run off the road.

Our van whips on up the road slinging its tail seemingly over the corners of dirt pathways reaching a point after 6 hours when I can tolerate no more. On one turn, with the river gorge a mere 1000 feet below, his wheels inches from the precipice and an on-coming car, I rise in protest. He had to slow down. Others seemed to agree. A blown tire would mean our death. Our Pakistani handler prevails upon him to slow down, which he so graciously does for 30 minutes. The remainder of this expedition becomes a mission for me to avoid dealing with the Karakoram Highway entirely. I would have to catch one of those elusive flights out of Skardu. Why they are so elusive remains a mystery to me throughout the trip. Scott and I have begun hatching multiple schemes to ensure avoidance of ever traveling this road again.

We overnight in a place called Chilas. It is an interesting hotel which is strangely reminiscent of a dungeon. The doors to our rooms lock from the outside with multiple fastening/deadbolt systems. I surmise this must have been a prison in a former capacity. It is also devoid of air conditioning, at least in my opinion. Brian disagrees with me. Some would say we had an argument. There is a large fan embedded in the wall and pointed directly at the window to the hallway. Brian thinks it is a primitive air conditioner. I assess it to be nothing more than a fan. He wants to close the room entirely, I do not. Having been sick all day on that road with the driver from Hell, I was in no mood for his air conditioner theory in the heat. We would sleep with the windows open and that was that. If there is one thing Brian cannot tolerate it is extreme heat. He is also quite confident that I am wrong and just being impatient. He is correct on the latter account but I briefly indulge his determination.

Closing all the windows to prove his point, the temperature rises to about 600 degrees and he still stubbornly insists it is cooling. My suppressed irritability allows no further toleration of this rationale and I depart for the dining room, which has to be cooler. Brian is behind me within three minutes. There we sit for a half hour prior to the meal in front of a huge fan that blows desert air over our heads. It isn't until after dinner, when we pass everyone else's room with their windows open and the fans blazing, that he concedes.

Little did we realize that this small town, with all the heat and jail cell rooms is an active hotbed of Taliban activity. It is much later on the trek when Balti porters informed me of the danger there and caution us about our return. This particular evening the only danger of which I am aware is re boarding that bus in the morning and finding bathrooms. My stomach issue abates with the dosage of some Cipro I had procured in Islamabad. I was starting to see some light at the end of the gut tunnel. We lay on top of bed sheets now thoroughly wet with perspiration through the night. Early the following morning after a light breakfast in the still hot dining room, we re-board the death machine for our final leg up the Karakoram Highway. Two men are sleeping in front of the hotel with automatic weapons lying across their laps. The driving is no better and in some ways much worse. It has to end at some point. Fortunately for me, the day proves somewhat shorter and we reach Skardu before dark. I manage not to have to make any emergency stops or heave out the window this day. We put 26 hours on those four wheels. I subtracted five years from my life. Quitting tobacco a decade ago seems like a wash.

SKARDU 6/13 ALTITUDE: 7545 FEET

Figure 5: Skardu on the Indus
Photo John Quillen

Pulling in to the Concordia Hotel, Brian and I make for the open lobby to snatch a key and ditch our companions. We occupy a spacious room overlooking the Indus River with beautiful mountain peaks surrounding our domicile. It is comfortable and rightly so. Beyond our knowledge, Skardu is to be home for almost one week, one unplanned week. The following day we arise, enjoy a pleasant breakfast at the hotel and walk over to the ATP office to sort, collect and manage gear for the trek up the glacier. This means assembling tents, climbing gear, ropes, fuel, emergency oxygen, first aid and sundries. It takes the better part of the day. Many of the tents are in desperate of repair. Brian and I set up about ten of them and mark their condition for repair as Scott and Ron filter through barrels for rope, pitons and emergency gear. I also spend time testing the solar charging apparatus. In the hot upper loft of ATP's compound in Skardu are shelves of expedition stores of past and present climbers. Future porters assist us as we trade broken tent poles for ripped vestibules. It is a jigsaw puzzle with piles of assorted tent pieces but this task is important. We need ten tents, two for each camp from one to three plus four spares. Rummaging through ATP's gear room, I spy a familiar name on one of the many duffel bags, Alexy Bolotov. Considering that he died on Everest two months prior, I wonder who would retrieve his belongings and what plans he had for the Karakoram before he tragically fell pursuing a new line on the world's highest peak.

Figure 6: Assembling expedition food in Skardu
Photo Brian Moran

Our group relaxes that evening and enjoys a nice dinner at the Concordia Motel. Nice in Pakistan means dhal, rice and some cucumber salad. We generally enjoy mango or watermelon for desert. I always have bottled water on the ready and sometimes would splurge the 60 rupees for a bottle of coke. Skardu seems like an outpost on the top of civilization's line. Gazing up the river, I imagine the glacial terminus upon which our team will soon be marching for over 100 miles following the big jeep ride. I harbor some trepidation about the potential discomforts of this next leg or two. It is hot enough here in this town but we would gain elevation daily. I imagine that would offset the intolerable sun from which we could not escape. We are getting to know each other and our Iranian teammates along with Ganga. I didn't realize how famous our fellow team member had become until we were standing together in the ATP office later and I spy a picture of her atop Everest's summit with the tag line, "**First *Mangolian* Woman to Summit Mt. Everest**". (*They may have mangled her name but the sentiment was implied as she adorned a wall with the likes of Uli Steck and Herman Buhl.*) Sharing a permit entails having the same base camp facilities. It means that we have meals together, hike up the glacier together and tent in close proximity. It is an amicable assemblage of climbers and none of us really give much thought to the idea that these guys are supposedly "enemies" of the United States. Like our North American contingent, these Persian counterparts seem to look beyond the media hyperbole.

The Iranians are a polite, entertaining troupe. They always defer to us when plates are passed or doors are held open. In particular is Aidin (pronounced Ideen). Age 25, he is a university student with decent English and a giant, toothy smile. Whenever we enter a door, Aidin stops and insists that Brian or I go first. Same with plates at meal time. No matter how many times I argue with him, he always ends with "*It's all right, no problem.*" I give up trying to argue with him about it. All of those Iranians are equally well-mannered. Hospitality means deferring to others. (*Subsequently, it was no problem for us to wait on their late arriving teammate, Ramin, who shows up two days after we arrive in Skardu.*)

Excited about the possibility of departing for Askole the following day, all slept well following the bus ride. Brian and I relax in our spacious room with excellent views and no air conditioning. I take a final shower. The next morning, however, news comes that our climbing permit has yet to be issued. Another delay means another day in Skardu. I don't think anyone minded. Skardu is a relaxing place. We could explore the town and secure more supplies. I depart on a quest for candy bars. Candy bars are .40 cents (*40 rupees*). Brian has some unknown business on the far side of town and proceeds to flag a Pakistani teenager on a motorcycle who pulls over and allows him to jump on back for a free ride into the inner sanctum of Skardu. We later visit the local mountaineering shop and see a beautiful down climbing suit. I couldn't help but wonder if it had not been peeled from some erstwhile mountaineer's corpse. Skardu is what I envision as true Pakistan. Donkey carts share the dirt streets with motorcycles and cars. Pedestrians are as common as afternoon dust storms. After reuniting some two hours later in the middle of town, Brian and I encounter a vehicle that heralds the owner as *"winner of all above 8000 meter peack."* Soon we are conversing with Hassan Sadpara.

Figure 7: Sadpara's exploits are advertised, by Sadpara
Photo John Quillen

Figure 8: Hassan Sadpara relates his attempts on the high peaks of Pakistan.
Photo John Quillen

Hassan is somewhat famous, as I later discover. He was the second Pakistani to summit all of his countries 8000 meter peaks and did so without supplemental oxygen. Hailing from the small Balti village from which he adopted his surname, Sadpara, Hassan never received a formal education but served as a porter for various mountaineering expeditions in the Karakoram. His first try on Broad Peak in 1996 resulted in an apex on the rocky foresummit, the true summit eluding him until 11 years later. As a result of his successes, the Pakistani government sponsored his ascent of Mt. Everest in 2011. Sadpara reached the top of the world, this time with supplemental oxygen to become the second Pakistani to ever reach earth's highest point. Sadpara runs a trekking service similar to ATP and tries to pry us away from our present arrangements. We respectfully decline but take his card anyway.

There is a K2 museum in town constructed by the Italian government. Shaped like a pyramid it has little to hold my attention from a mountaineering standpoint. The lazy afternoons I spend jogging down on the river bed where the sand made a soft strip of cushioned track for my aging joints. Dropping down the quarter mile to the water, I pass small mud huts where women tend goats with their children. At my approach, they turn to cover their faces as I navigate a porous pathway to the water. Occasionally I become aware of young men spying on me at the river bank late in the day. On two occasions I am approached by curious locals anxious to test their English on a foreigner. Shortly into the conversations comes the inevitable, "*Where from?*"

I would reply "US". This affects a reply of dropped smile and slung head. On both occasions the disappointed locals slunk off, however politely. Drone strikes may have killed one of their cousins, for all I knew.

We rejoin for dinner at the hotel and what we think to be our final night of leisure in Skardu. The eight hour jeep ride to Askole is much anticipated.

Ron, from his previous foray to K2 makes us aware that is to be the most thrilling four-wheel drive adventure of our lives. I can only draw from the Karakoram highway experience and push the thoughts from my head. From Askole we will begin the 10-day backpack to Broad Peak base camp. Ron is an interesting fellow, who, judging from his history, climbs solo most of the time. He is an upbeat and positive guy who is figuring out the expedition leading role into which he was so unexpectedly thrust. I never asked him specifically how he was chosen for this task but assumed it involved some free climbing on some level. Like many of us would, he likely jumped at an opportunity when presented.

I spy a couple of new arrivals at the Concordia and quickly recognize one of them as Bruce Normand. It is quite ironic that I run into this guy because two years ago, while travelling to the other side of this mountain range in China I become acquainted with his climbing partner, Kyle Dempster as we shared adjoining seats from Seattle to Beijing. If neither of these names ring a bell, then I suggest looking in to what they did to receive the Piolet D'or, alpinism's Holy Grail of mountaineering for their ascent of Xuelin's North Wall. After listening to him speak in that Scottish accent I wait a day to make sure before introducing myself. One of Bruce's many claims to fame is that he successfully summited K2 in an epic ascent, thus making him the 264th person to have ever accomplished that particular feat. I spend many hours listening to him recount that harrowing tale which is well documented in the Shared Summits video from 2007. Bruce and his team were here to climb some little known, likely never ascended peak somewhere near Paiyu. We spend several afternoons in the courtyard of the Concordia Motel. One of his team mates is an American named Jesse Mease who is a former navy man who traded his gun for pitons and ice screws. Jesse is a super nice guy along with all of Normand's international troupe. Bruce enjoys relating the K2 story almost as much as I am regaled by it.

THE PERMIT PROBLEM

Another day brings another delay. The Gilgit- Baltistan counsel is delaying our climbing permit for reasons unknown. Now on our second day, the delay is, for me, anyway, just an excuse to remain inactive. Still recovering from the stomach issue I do not lament additional rest opportunity. Scott and Brian seem somewhat uncomfortable and I sense a bit of general anxiety over the delay; I was not at that point, yet. Any excuse for laziness is readily accepted.

The third day, however, a general discontent festers and swells. Questions are asked at the ATP office. Brian and I make a foray over there early in the morning to inquire of Nick Nam, ATP office manager. To our surprise, it is suggested that this all is a result of Field Touring changing the name of the trip leader at the last minute. Ron was a replacement for Chris Szymiec. Chris was friends with Brian, they had climbed Aconcagua together several years prior. He was a large part of the motivation to use FTA. When we were informed of his removal from the lineup three weeks prior to the trip, it wasn't a great concern. We were already prepared to depart and figured the adjustments and replacement leader would be appropriate. Now confronted with this new information, some concern is justified. More days of delay will cut into our climbing time. It isn't at critical mass yet but could be soon.

Back at the hotel where Wi-Fi is as intermittent as hot water, we email Field Touring. Their indignation about the problem having to do with them is evident. A couple more days and a couple more delays means that the rhetoric and banter rises to heightened levels via email and phone calls to FTA. FTA could not believe that ATP is laying the blame on them and fingers are crossing in all directions We end up delayed for a total of six days in Skardu—a warranted concern considering our climbing window. At one point all team members, including the Iranians, assemble at ATP offices to demand answers. Naik Nam Karim, ATP Skardu manager, insists that it is out of his hands. There was little doubt this was now cutting into climbing days. Little did I realize that this was just the first week long period of waiting we would endure before journey's end.

Our Iranian/American/Canadian/Chinese Broad Peak team makes a first group decision. We will pursue a trekking permit in the meantime that allows us to begin our advance to base camp. Our hope is that the climbing permit will be issued as we meander towards the Baltoro glacier. I am somewhat skeptical. One week was incredibly long, even by Pakistani standards, according to ATP. In reference to the FTA involvement and likely mishandling of documentation leading to this snafu, I am told by FTA owner Dave Hancock in Australia, *"If it were me and I were 25 years old, I would smile, wink and climb the peak anyway."*

My response to his email was such, *"Since I am 47 years old and possessed of more wisdom and an aversion to Pakistani prisons, I will pass."* It is somewhat inconceivable to me that the owner of this company was even making a suggestion that we engage in an illegal activity in Pakistan. Nevertheless, we proceed towards the Karakoram via our land cruiser limousines the following day. I tell Brian *"The journey has to carry us day by day."* Two hours into the bumpy ride we reach a village named Shigar; the road is blocked by rock fall. Ron conveys this will add two hours' time to our trip. We take lunch in the dirtiest restaurant I have ever seen. There was no way I could consume anything from this pig sty. Of course, the Iranians are undeterred and dive right into the dhal and rice, drinking from glasses that were cloudier than the sky. I shoe flies from my face and wonder what food will look like on the trek. Erroneously I assume that the worst of my stomach issues has been endured.

Some of the bridges our land cruiser negotiate are missing planks so that at times, only three wheels of the Toyotas are on firm footing. The jeeps drive up and over boulders and into ravines with ease. A strange noise is successfully diagnosed by our Balti chauffeur with a lug wrench as he stops to tighten one of the wheels. I am seated on the front seat in the left side of the land cruiser. Behind me are Azim, an Iranian, and Brian. (*Brian named Azim the "Silver Fox" because of his thick head of grey hair and our inability to differentiate Arab names. It seemed as if everyone in this part of the world had some appellation that is a variant of the name Aziz, or Azim or Asim. In his late fifties, Azim is always smiling and we have yet to ascertain his connection with the other Iranians.*) Through the rearview I glance as we hit ditch after ditch to see Azim and Brian's heads simultaneously bounce off the vehicle ceiling. Scowls and mouths full of dust decry a poor choice of seating. I can feel their disdain burning a hole through the back of my head as I sip water from a bottle disingenuously offering to trade places.

Figure 9: This was our "Limo" for 10 hours. The nomenclature, well…
Photo Brian Moran

We pass through villages that rarely see vehicles unless they are carrying trekkers on seasonal migration. Dark skinned children reach out for our hands as we weave through small hamlets. A military outpost requires that our caravan of three jeeps stop while we are inspected by a group of shady looking characters wearing jump suits like characters from a mafia series. Again, fears of Taliban creep into my head. Could they have erected this "checkpoint" to find American scalps? They didn't look like any policeman I have ever seen. I find out later from our liaison officer, that these guys are an army unit. Army units in Pakistan wear jump suits and gold chains. *(We encounter another group similarly dressed later in the trip.)* Deeming us no safety risk they wave our vehicle on through but not before handing our driver a dead chicken to ferry to someone up the road.

Figure 10: Negotiating rivers on moving planks
Photo John Quillen

It is nearly dark when we reach Askole. Palpable is the feeling of relief shared by all who are itching to ditch the machine made dust storms for a self-propelled variety. ATP has a building there with tent spots. We are introduced to our cook staff and "guide". Aside from sharing the name of many cartoon protagonists from my childhood in the 70s, "Zoltan" is to be the ringleader of all things from this point forward. Every bag, porter, donkey, goat and dzo is his responsibility. Our cook, Sher Ali, prepares a first meal prior to a 5 a.m. departure. It is a shadow of things to come, eggs, hard-boiled.

Figure 11: Moonlight over Askole village with snowcapped peaks shadowing our first encampment
Photo Brian Moran

I sleep well this evening and poke my head out of the tent to see my breath in the early dawn. At five a.m. we are roused for a breakfast of hot, powdered milk and more hard-boiled eggs. My three bags loaded with climbing gear, food and clothing are laid out in the compound for porters to disperse. At six a.m. we commence our march on the road. Our trek meanders alongside the Indus River and begins, auspiciously enough, at the end of ATP's compound in Askole.

This day begins crisp but soon turns hot. We enter a line of Balti Porters saddled with luggage, tents, kitchen supplies and goats. Some carry live, chirping chickens that are, unbeknownst to me, slated for dinner that evening in Jhola, our first campsite. Brian and I saunter unhurried, no stranger to these kinds of approaches. The increasing heat of this unfolding day sees our pace slacken even more. The walk is along sandy, river moraine that is gently sloped and never out of the constantly blaring sun. Donkeys and mules are constant companions along with their detritus. It is a conga line of supplies all going in one direction.

JHOLA

10,334 feet June 21, 2013

This outpost comes into view after ten hours of unbearable heat hiking. I round the bend of an elbow in the river basin and spot blue buildings that I later discover are toilets. It is deceptive because I still have well over one hour of hiking before I will cross the river on a rope bridge and turn back to this place that is less than a quarter mile as the crow flies. A figure comes running up behind me and starts talking in his limited English. This baseball cap wearing, mustached young man is smiling and asks, "*Back happy?*" That takes me a minute to realize he is offering to carry my daypack. Muhammid Ali and I are fast friends and I soon learn he is part of our kitchen staff for the expedition. It is nearing 3.30 p.m. and no escape from the sun is available. We make the collective mistake of advancing beyond our supply chain. This means having to wait for tents and food in the blistering heat. There isn't but one shade tree in the whole campsite and many, many people competing for its respite. Brian is crouched with the Iranians in the doorway of some edifice that seems to have no particular function.

Other trekkers have established tents already. We wait until almost dark for our army to arrive but once there, make quick work of setting up our compound and dining facility. The only thing missing is my naughty big bag, again. Of the two that did survive, one is shredded beyond usage. It has obviously been attached to a donkey and rubbed constantly against something to the point that there is a hole the size of a big head. That "*big head hole*" strangely matches the dimensions of my climbing helmet poking halfway through. Unfortunately, it was attached to stock instead of porters on the first leg of the journey. Those big blue barrels Ron and Scott spent such effort to procure in Skardu were starting to make sense. Ron's experience trekking to K2 had proven that the ardors of the trail lent itself

29

to gear damage. He had the forethought to place our solar charging equipment and sensitive electronics in that sturdy container. Thankfully nothing fell out of my blue bag, that I notice.

In the big bag, however, is my sleeping kit. Its lack of arrival means no sleeping amenities. By the time Zoltan arrives later, and I inform him of the oversight, his seeming lack of concern ignites me. By dinner, I am tiring and ready to lie down, I still have no bag or sleeping pad. I go off on Zoltan in front of the group; my patience exhausted. How am I expected to sleep without a bag or pad? Zoltan assures me it will arrive. I emphasize that I have to have sleeping gear, he insists that I wait. I insist that he will move up a glacier without a sleeping bag, more than once.

Nevertheless, I make do with a borrowed bag and no pad. Next morning at six a.m., my gear arrives as I am setting off towards the next camp at Paiyu, a 12-hour walk. I can't tell you the mileage. Internet searches give varying amounts of the total trek from 100 miles to 130. I can tell you that I walk at least 2.5 miles per hour and 12 hours would seem to be at least 20 but things are different at altitude and in Pakistan.

Figure 12: Blaring sun required early starts and diligent hydration.
Photo John Quillen

SLEEPING IN THE SLAUGHTER HOUSE

Paiyu 11,417 feet June 22, 2013

Paiyu is a figural place. It is here that we are to take a rest day. I have sweated so much that my shirt can stand by itself. A ring of residual perspiration colors my sun cap nearly solid white with salt. This is the only day that I beat Brian into camp. He is a full hour behind trying to stave off the potential for overheating by walking in a strange, very slow rhythm. Brian is fanatic about heat, you would never think he is a Georgia boy. When I come rolling in, Muhammid Ali, hands me a warm cup of tea and produces a seat in the shade where our tents were soon erected. (*I should say after the donkeys were finished defecating on the platform areas. I was becoming very annoyed with the lack of separation between pack stock and humans.*) For whatever reason, Muhammid takes it upon himself to perform as a personal assistant for me and Brian. I sit down next to Ramin in the sweltering June oven beneath the shade of some unknown type of tree sipping black tea with lots of sugar. Disparate as it sounds, the respite is a pure delight.

Brian comes rolling in equally desperate for water and also manages to choke down this hot tea until they can boil enough drinking water for the group. Ramin and I speak of his days in Tehran and present life in Canada. I discover that he is a student of mountaineering literature and martial arts. Ramin had served in the Iranian Army during his twenties. He and I are the same age. I think about what I was doing in my twenties and appreciate the lack of draft that would have seen me in a similar circumstance. He fought in border areas against the Kurds, I fought my parents over whether or not I could buy parachute pants. Several porters passed by our area making weird chants. Over and over they trade this seemingly nonsensical greeting reminiscent of middle schoolers taunting each other. Before long, when our liaison officer, returns, Ramin asks, "*What means la la lal lla la?*" And that is exactly how it sounded when those Baltis uttered the phrase over and over. But to hear it from Ramin with his slight Farsi accent tickled me. And I start laughing uncontrollably. Yawer has no explanation. He is, by Pakistani standards, a wealthy city boy from Islamabad. He then explains how he cannot converse with the Baltis in their native dialect. Dinner that night sees us tearing into our chirping companions along the trail. It is a really fresh chicken dish that really doesn't taste like chicken, mixed in a brown stew of some sort. Knowing we are exempted from having to walk the following day, Brian and I crawl into our shared tent and pass out until the first rays of morning dawn peacefully in defiance of events elsewhere.

On this rest day we do laundry and take a bucket bath. That means getting some hot water from the cook staff, walking down to the toilet area with some soap, lathering up and sparingly rinsing. I was scraping salt from every pore of by body and the result is a feeling that I have shed several pounds. I have no towel and it doesn't matter, the noonday sun dries my pink flesh, much to the likely chagrin of Ganga, who endures the unfortunate experience of witnessing my emergence from the "shower" stall half naked. We soon learn that many animals have been on a one way trip to this place. Most every goat and chicken we had followed and passed meets their demise here. I lose count of how many animals fulfill their ultimate destiny at Paiyu. Watching them slaughtered is a past time for many Westerners. Watching us watch them slaughter goats is a past time for the Balti staff. As a result of the ensuing carnage and detritus, we rename Paiyu to "*Peeyu*".

Figure 13: Aiden seeks shade for a shave at Paiyu.
Photo Scott Powrie

Ron and Scott decide that it is my turn to send out an audio dispatch for the Field Touring expedition blog. Ron had made one or two from Skardu and I think it would be a good opportunity to say hello to everyone back home on Field Touring's dime. I was told later that my voice sounded exhausted and high pitched and folks were worried. They thought I was aware of the news from over the mountain. Ron waits until I am finished with the satellite phone transmission to deliver it. "*11 people have been killed on Nanga Parbat.*" When Ron said there was bad news from that mountain I instinctively reference the usual mountaineering maladies such as avalanche and crevasses. He whispers while gently taking the bulky satellite phone from my hand. Taliban dressed as police walked into base camp there and systematically executed 11 aspirant mountaineers. It was incredible information.

I remembered reading a story from 2008 where German trekkers were moving through the area and asked their handlers how to identify Taliban. The staff of their trekking agency laughed and, allegedly said, "*We are Taliban*". For all we knew, our porters were Taliban. As Ron relates the tragedy on Nanga Parbat I think of my friends and family now glued to the international news outlets. What fear must now be instilled as a result of this action. We seek word of Tunc Findic. It is very likely that he has been among the victims. Our team asks questions of our liaison officer and Zoltan who confirms the news but can give us no information on Tunc. Throughout that last evening, every noise outside of our tent is a potential Taliban incursion.

Figure 14: Muhammid Ali prepares dinner.
Photo Brian Moran

As if in keeping with the terror theme we are subsequently exposed to Balti rituals involving chanting and beating of drums throughout the second night. It is tribal, primitive and suggestive of Africa headhunting, in my mind anyway. We are caught by surprise when, at dusk, a slow, methodical banging on one of the metal barrels lying about is followed by a rising cacophony of synchronous drumming. This goes on for ten minutes before the chanting ensues. At first the chants are seemingly random, like a musician warming his instrument. Soon every porter in the compound is unified in a chorus of guttural, hair raising vocal eruption. It lasts for hours. Neither Brian nor I can ignore the obvious coincidental timing of this tribal event. Our minds race back and forth from Paiyu to Nanga Parbat with varying scenarios. We have little choice but to pray that their Balti chants do not signify any suggestion with regard to the sacrifice of Western infidels. I seriously consider gathering my sleeping kit and sneaking up the hill to lay down for the remainder of the night. If something happens, I don't want to be a sleeping duck. Fortunately, exhaustion displaces fear and we are both soon dead asleep instead of just dead.

The chanting ritual is repeated the following evening in Urdukas, renamed Doo Dookas by us because of the omnipresent pack stock leavings. Pakistanis make no differentiation between pack stock areas and people areas. It creates quite the problem but lack of hygiene was something with which I am continually forced to contend. Having watched our cook staff cut the throats of chicken and proceed to pound out chapattis by hand with no washing in between is getting to be the norm. I will not mention other hygienic oversights in the same "vein".

URDUKAS

Figure 15: Urdukas Camp
Photo Ramin Shojaei

Urdukas (Doodookas) is a strange place on the side of a hill. Another super-hot, 100 degree plus day of backpacking and ten hours deposits us at this place. Our guide printed from FTA rates this day as "moderate". I strongly disagree. It is, without a doubt, the most strenuous and steep of the trek. We cross great boulder fields and traipse across the river floor. In several places the trail is faint and Brian and I pick through, route finding over giant boulders that rise up to 20 feet from the ground. I imagine the trouble if one of us were to twist an ankle or mis-step off one of these giant rocks. I wear tennis shoes for the entire journey. The heat was creating monumental blisters for Scott and Brian so I intend to avert the ovens that would become those boots. It was a risk but the tradeoff is breathability and success on the blister front. Scott loses half the skin off his heel because he is wearing his mountaineering boots for the trek. Like others, he expected to confront glacial features and not endure this Bataan death march through indescribable heat.

One successful idea I have, pardon the back patting, is to bring my water filter. I don't know how we would have survived without it. To average ten hours of hiking per day on just the water you can carry is a stretch. I drink a lot of water. Brian drinks twice as much as me. They told me that I had better be proficient with a water filter to make potable aqua from the silty rivers we followed to our destination. I sought creeks that ran into the river and make attempts to let it settle before filtering. This system performs advantageously, much to the curious amazement of Balti porters who simply lift an empty food can and replace it for their successors upon a rock near our filtering stations. Understand that water from the cook tents is boiled. It does nothing for the silt and remains warm all day. Water from glacial streams is cold and refreshing. My Katadyn hiker pro performs admirably. *(By the time we reach base camp, I had filtered several dozen gallons for the two of us. It was at this time that the filter became irrevocably clogged, having made do until the bitter end.)* How folks could hike for 12 hours on some days with just 3 quarts of water was beyond me. I drank, and drank and drank. Two of our group suffers heat exhaustion. One of them is our liaison officer.

Speaking of the liaison officer, let me explain. He is a military attaché "loaned" to us for political and economic reasons. For that privilege our expedition will pay him $1500 for trekking gear plus a daily allowance and all the dhal and boiled eggs he could stomach. Yawer Ashafaq is his name and we get along famously. He is a captain in the Pakistani army. At 24 years old he harbors ambitions of climbing alongside our group on Broad Peak; never mind that he possesses no climbing experience. None. Yawer's determination is both admirable and frightening. *(He also accrued a severe case of heat stroke on the first day's walk to Jhola. Yawer was sporting a new fleece jacket zipped all the way up to his neck. It was at least 100 degrees and likely more. I kept quizzing him about this layering strategy but he had a plan. I don't believe that vomiting was part of his plan. It was a nice fleece, though.)*

Another strange and eerie story regarding Urdukas is the event that occurred there in August of 2011. Straddling a boulder filled hill, this camping area is flanked by huge rocks that appear ready to crush climbing parties. On one fateful day it did just that, killing 3 porters and permanently entombing them on the site. We lay just feet from a rock that sits on top of multiple dead porters and their tents, or what is left of them, is sticking out from the sides. It was like taking a gumball, wrapping it in a handkerchief and stuffing it into a bottle. Death and reminders thereof are becoming more frequent as we pick our way up to the snout of the Baltoro glacier.

Figure 16: Fires commemorate a religious observance.
Photo Ramin Shojaei

Urdukas is, as previously mentioned, the sight of more Olympic chanting by the porters. Following dinner I am summoned by Ramin outside the dining tent. In the fading twilight there are small fires lit throughout the camp which create an eerie, solemn scene. Ramin conveys that this is in commemoration of a powerful Imam's birthday. It heralds an evening of worship and chanting which lasts for about 2 hours during prime sleep time. Bellowing is a cantor and 30 respondents to his chants. In unison they wail to the Heavens. In my tent, I wail into a pillow.

THE GREATEST MUSEUM OF SHAPE AND FORM:

Goro 2 14,763 feet June 25, 2013

Figure 17: Cathedrals rise from the snout of the Baltoro.
Photo John Quillen

Figure 18: Crisp mornings herald our approaching glacier.
Photo John Quillen

Italian Fosco Maraini was a mountaineer who photographed the Karakoram extensively in the years before most of the world even knew of its existence. It was his designation that referred to the trek into the Baltoro glacier as the *"Greatest museum of shape and form on earth."* Since we are under the gun time wise, the decision is made to speed up our trek to base camp and shorten the ten day trip to six. OK, I am not one to rush things but such is the will of the group. It means that we will skip campsites and double mileage on certain days. As a result we would only experience one more campsite, Goro 2, and then shoot past Concordia to Broad Peak. I was in shape but this pace didn't lend much to my personal form. Neither did it confer anticipated opportunity to make my own personal photographic journal.

This stretch to Goro 2 is undoubtedly the most pleasant leg of the trek. Maybe that is due to the fact that we only hike for six and a half hours and the giant peaks of Masherbrum and the Great Trango Towers come into view. I am alone and enjoying the transition from boulders to gravel. As the sun rotates to its apex in the skyline I am more appreciative of what Pouya, the young Iranian went out of his way to do for me this morning. In my rush to get moving up the trail, I left my sun hat in the dining tent. A quarter mile up from Urdukas camp site I am brushing my teeth when he comes running to me with it. Pouya doesn't speak a lick of English and smiles as he hands the nasty, sweat encrusted head covering to me just about the time I have realized it was gone. He saves me an additional half mile of walking this day. (*Later in camp I fish for one of the remelted candy bars and give him a deformed Kit Kat. He first waves his hand in refusal but I insist. He understands that is the only way I have to thank him.*) Elevation gains are gradual and a crispness gives hint of the approaching snow.

At Goro 2 a couple of things occur. The porters have established our tent right where the trail comes in from the north, unbeknownst to us. After dinner, Brian and I retire early. He has the capital idea of setting up his iPhone for some program viewing compliments of a downloaded PBS special from iTunes. It confers a sense of home and we set up in our tent for a bit of Americana. It is comforting and Western. Having a "television" lends some "civilization" to this place. We forget about being so far from everything. Our domicile is warm and safe.

Within two minutes of starting the video our tent shakes with a violent uproar and we are nearly upended.

"What the hell is that?

Brian yells as nylon and flesh smack the side of my face; our home rapidly deforms from what I can only surmise is an earthquake or worse. I am rolled towards his side of the tent where he is fighting to extricate himself from the comforts of his sleeping bag. A huge commotion ensues outside with a mixture of human and animal sounds. As it turns out, donkeys, fresh from their rotation to Concordia, become entangled in our nylon dwelling's guy-outs. They apparently did not expect a tent on their trail either. (*Our high altitude porter, Aziz, was responsible for tent placement throughout this journey and this wasn't to be the first time it becomes a major issue*) It appears as if they will fall on top of us and we will suffer a fate similar to the porters at Urdukas. I set a record springing from my sleeping bag as the weight of the animals bears down upon us. I lurch from the tent in time to shoo the remaining pack stock who are equally surprised with this late night obstacle. Nevertheless, the damage is done. I spend half an hour erecting rocks as a barrier around our tent to prevent subsequent maladies. Sleep is now quite elusive but it really matters not since we are awakened at 4 a.m. anyway.

It is becoming quite routine that the porters will hit the trail super early to avoid this heat. As a result it means that they wish to pack up our tents to square their loads. Never mind that breakfast is a full hour away. This day dawns cool, below freezing as a matter of fact. Brian and I roll out grumpy as you would expect from a bunch of trampled mountaineers. In addition, we are both coming down with another stomach bug that dogs us for the remainder of the day's walk. That's a shame because on this day is the much anticipated entrance to Concordia.

As I am again suffering another or perhaps same, mutated version of gastrointestinal delight, my pace is slowest of the bunch. Moving upward we encounter a phenomena known as ice ships. These "ships" rise from the glacier to create surreal sculptures that have fin shapes or sails. Some reach 50 feet in height. My only present use for them is to serve as a barrier between me and the porters as I crouch and seek multiple relief breaks due to the aforementioned malady. Even Brian is well ahead as I make multiple stops and "scout for snow leopards". Being sick on a bus on the Karakoram Highway is probably the most heinous of situations. Gaining elevation on the Baltoro while wrenching in stomach pain in blistering heat is likely next on the suffer fest list.

I had particularly anticipated this section of trail cognizant that this branch will bring the full range of the Karakoram's eight thousand meter peaks into view. I force myself, although miserable, to snap dozens of breathtaking photographs. In my head are walls in my house that will showcase these indescribable mountainous landscapes perfectly. In six and a half hours I spy Concordia and the split of the glacier. There are tents in the distance and to the right is the Gasherbrum group, to the left is Broad Peak and K2. I am standing in the place of which I have imagined in my dreams and all I am able to think about are the dirty hands of our cook staff and everyone touching chapattis with their unwashed appendages.

CONCORDIA, THRONE ROOM OF THE MOUNTAIN GODS

15,255 feet

Figure 19: K2 dominates the Karakoram skyline
Photo Scott Powrie

I will never forget my first true glimpse of K2. The weather is clear and she has a small cloud ringing 26,000 feet, right at camp 4. Before me is the mountain of all mountains, a peak I have studied for decades often wondering if it would live up to the photography. It does not take my breath away, the atmosphere is doing that sufficiently here at nearly 15,000 feet. K2 is the most beautiful, perfectly sculpted peak in the world. She shadows you in myriad majestic and daunting ways. Immediately apparent are the danger, allure and siren like attraction. K2 rises from the Karakoram skyline, a giant among the grandest structures on earth. She is the queen of the ball, the debutante of the town and the ruler of all mountains holding court high above everything. If Concordia is the throne room then K2 bears the scepter from which our objective, Broad Peak drapes the right shoulder. K2 is, in local tongue, known as Chogori, which means *"King of Mountains"*. I have no difficulty channeling the emotion that led climber/photographer Galen Rowell to formulate the appellation *"Throne Room of the Mountain Gods."*

K3, our mountain, appears no less daunting. Flanking the right shoulder of a panorama this royal sibling is all that separates this rocky, alien land from China. Broad Peak is a jagged, multiple spiked mother that doesn't grin at all. She is a scowling mountain with her nose up in the air, warning all who consider mounting her. I don't feel any animosity towards me personally from Broad Peak but I detect anger from that mountain that will be requited. I realize this sounds strange but Broad Peak feels as if she has an axe to grind with someone. I'm not sure why. Perhaps it is the awareness of what transpired in the winter of this year when she claimed the lives of two Polish mountaineers whose bodies were yet to be discovered. It is as if Broad Peak is saying, *"Yeah, lust after my beautiful sibling, but I'm the one with whom you had better be concerned!"*

Figure 20: Broad Peak aka K3
Photo Brian Moran

I turn left at Concordia for what I hope will be a short walk into Broad Peak base camp. That short walk turns into 3 more hours of boulder hopping and some rappelling down snow slopes over rivers of flowing water. I wasn't expecting this level of adventure until well after base camp but it makes me forget about my stomach issue for a few hours as I grab ancient telephone wire cables to arm rappel over seemingly bottomless caverns of ice.

It is an endless slog into base camp and no member of my expedition, including the 100 plus porters, donkeys, goats and dzo are to be seen. I resort to doing that thing I hate so much, asking returning porters *"How far is Broad Peak base camp?"* Their stock answer is always, *"One hour"*. If they know any English, that is the phrase. Over the next four hours I receive the same answer from four different, returning Baltis. I am really flagging now by the time I spot the first of our orange tents in the distance. When I reach base camp the sun is setting.

Being last into camp means I get the crappiest home assignment compliments of Aziz again, right below the mess tent. On top of that, our cook, Sher Ali, decides to dig out a water hole about 5 feet from the front vestibule of my tent. A small argument ensues between Ron and head cook, Sher Ali regarding this choice of water procurement. Ron holds up a pitcher of grey silt and suggests they walk further from camp for a better source. Sher Ali proclaims, "*I am cook, very professional.*" Unfortunately, Sher Ali prevails and we were forced to contend with an extra dose of daily fiber. (*Cook staff were digging for water every day at sunup just outside my sleeping quarters.*) It really doesn't matter. I am so exhausted that I collapse inside the tent for an hour without a bag or sleeping pad. Just to lie horizontally is such a relief that all else pales. It is June 26, 2013. We have walked over 100 miles and I am feeling every one of them as I lay on the bare floor of my new home for the next 6 weeks with my legs rolling up into my chin. I want to sit outside and bask in the glorious radiance of K2. Rumblings from my stomach portend a turbulent night, so it doesn't happen.

Figure 21: My tent is on the moving glacier beside the watering hole.
Photo Brian Moran

By dinnertime I rally and join our expedition in the mess tent. There is Ron and Scott, Brian and Ganga, the Mongolian. Then of course are all the festive Iranians. They really are jovial guys. Always laughing and sometimes singing, they know how to make the best of all situations. Ramin has emerged as the obvious group leader and at 47, a seasoned climber. I grow close to Ramin as he is a very level headed and wise mountain guy. Similarly, Azim Behrmani, the "*Silver Fox*" is a guy in his late 50s who has quite a bit of climbing experience. One of his tasks on this trip is to place a memorial plaque on G2 for his climbing mate who perished there three years ago. Apparently, they were descending from camp when his friend fell off the side of the mountain to his death. Azim is a Broad Peak climber, though. He climbed on his own schedule and was not part of the Iranian attempt to put up a new route on Broad. That is for the young guns, Aidin, Pouya and Mojtaba. The only other character in the Iranian cast is Afshin Saadi. He is quick to pat you on the back, give a hug or convey a smile. His warmth and amiable nature make him definitely one of the more colorful members in our assemblage.

Figure 22: Pouya (left) Mojtaba (center) Aidin on trek to basecamp.
Photo John Quillen

I try to eat what I can and retire for an early night. My stomach grumbles with the presentation of rice and dhal. It does seem to give indication of abating, though. Now I can focus on the climb; we still don't have a permit and dinnertime discussions center on that fact. Our departure from Skardu was on a conditional trekking permit in hopes of securing a climbing permit. To date, no permit has materialized. Naik Naim from the Skardu ATP office was going to radio us when that occurred. Daily we inquire of Tunc Findic and news from Nanga Parbat. In this era of satellite technology, we remain woefully uninformed.

FOLLOW YOUR GUT

Broad Peak Base Camp 15,000 feet June 27, 2013

Sometime during the night I am confronted with the need to evacuate the contents of my stomach, again. Crawling from rock to rock in the shadow of K2 and K3 in the cold of this altitude I start making mental calculations about how much this trip is costing me per day, which is ridiculous. As if that somehow will improve my health or present mood. It is obvious that my statements of health were premature as I relapsed badly on the stomach virus to the point of total tent boundness by this particular day. I am having a fever and chills accompanied by requisite regurgitory functions. It is full on misery and I am enduring a prolonged suffer fest of epic proportion. No food will stay down, including crackers and the new altitude, 15000 feet is only exacerbating matters. I begin Cipro again, this time two days' worth. Laying in my tent, I miss three meals. Drifting in and out of fevers within minutes, flashes of dirty hands pounding rolls of dough hammer my dehydrated brain.

Proximity dictates that I can hear all conversations from our team in the mess tent, though, always drifting back to the permit, or lack thereof. A general discontent filters through this group and rightfully so. Consider that each person paid approximately seven thousand dollars (more for us Americans) and the financial investment alone was almost one hundred thousand dollars from the group. That is big money for ATP and Field Touring Alpine for the four of us. I knew how long the preparations for this expedition took in my world. The Iranians had been planning this new route for years, since their first attempt in 2009. They had some corporate sponsorship and the eyes of their countrymen and the world climbing community were upon them. Similarly, Ganga was representing Mongolia with her Broad Peak/K2 double-header plan. To turn around due to lack of a permit at this point was really just beyond comprehension for most of our "team".

As expected, our Yawer, is put on the spot with suggestion of climbing permit less. As military attaché, his job was to ensure rules were followed. Understandable is his reticence to indulge talk of "outlaw" climbing on this peak. The conversation turns into a full-blown argument between team members and Yawer as I lay on my side in the tent. I indulge more immediate concerns such as finding a pee bottle and making it to the rocks in time before heaving yet again. I overhear a suggestion that they sign a waiver for him if they climb without a permit. I dismiss the irrationality of these proposals as I slouch breathlessly, yet again, towards the tent's rear vestibule in this thin air at an altitude almost one thousand feet higher than any place in the continental United States.

Figure 23: Affable liaison officer, Yawer.
Photo John Quillen

Within an hour, Ron, Scott and Brian encircle my quarantine area. They are carrying the conversation to me and asking my opinion about signing this waiver to climb. Immediately I am stricken with the incredulity of this proposal and any notion that they could suggest such a thing. I was sick and not really in the mood to pursue the discourse. It brought me back to my email with FTA owner, Dave Hancock, in Skardu wherein he suggested I climb without a permit as well. Ron and Scott were saying that they probably intended to sign the waiver and Brian was leaning in their direction. My tolerance of this discussion reaches an end and I exclaim *"I am not signing a waiver because we don't have a permit. We are in freaking Pakistan, not the USA, have you forgotten where you are?"*

It is apparent that my protestations are falling on deaf ears. It doesn't matter what I say, these guys have climbing fever. None of my rationale was getting past the nylon of my tent. Between the stressors of the Nanga Parbat incident, our 100 miles of hell and this permit problem we did deserve a chance. My last comment on the subject is this, *"I tend to believe that things happen for a reason, have y'all considered that perhaps it is not meant for us to climb this mountain?"*

Ron seems a little moved by this but not for long. Scott isn't paying attention and Brian is making mental calculations about climbing rotations. I am immediately concerned about my climbing team and their unbridled summit ambitions. I end the conversation with my position clearly outlined. They depart intent upon subverting the permit "problem".

Brian and I chat afterward as Ron and Scott retire for the evening. Brian seems to reel himself in a bit after I jump on him and confront his seeming indiscretion. It is a human tendency. From a distance I witness 10 adults do the same thing so Brian snaps to and says, *"I really don't think I am going to climb without a permit either."* Brian relates to Ron this piece of information and has him convey it to FTA and ATP. This seems the most logical course of action. He then settles into his tent as we retire in our respective thoughts. During the night, explosive avalanches break from the unclimbed shoulders of K3. There are initial cracking noises followed by sonic booms waking us all. The very ground beneath shifts as if an earthquake has stirred. It seems like our mountain is coughing.

June 28, 2013

I begin to rally and feel like a human after the fever passes this morning. This is one day that I refuse to suffer in quarantined misery: that is for any other day of the year but my birthday. Coincidentally, following all this conversation and argument over the permit in the mess tent, we are informed by Zoltan and Ron that the permit has been issued sometime during the night like magic. Unbridled exuberance spills about the compound. Ramin and the Iranians have already made for camp 1 at sunup and radio that evening. (*It was apparent that they were marching on regardless and had few scruples about foreign red tape*) Still, they are relieved with the news as we all huddled around the radio for a scheduled check in at 6 p.m. I can hear the young guys shouting in the background. They also were in on the little secret that unfolds. After dinner was cleared from the table I am treated to a great surprise which Brian has apparently arranged. Sher Ali manufactures a birthday cake for me on my 47th anniversary of life. It is a very special touch. To have our permit and start feeling better all on the same day are the best presents imaginable. Brian and I formulate a plan to attack the hill the day after tomorrow. That should give me sufficient time to recuperate. Happiness creeps back into the throne room for a while.

Figure 24: My birthday celebration at base camp, June 28 2013. Sher Ali is far left. Behind him is our high altitude porter, Aziz.
Photo Brian Moran

CROSSING THE PALACE MOAT

June 30, 2013

Figure 25: Brian crosses the bridge of death.
Photo John Quillen

From our base camp It takes a full hour and a half just to get to the base of Broad Peak. You must cross the glacial river several times, weave through penitents (penitents are ice formations like the "ships" that are much smaller) and climb up and over several snow mounds before negotiating a big, rocky hill to reach the base of K3. It is really quite treacherous just reaching the start of the fixed line. You will get lost if not following someone there the first time and after that, the route changes as the very few wands get knocked down by moving ice.

As we depart that morning around 9 a.m., I shoulder a fully laden 50lb pack. The rebound from my illness imparts a great feeling of strength that is to be short lived once I reached the exertion of the icefall crossings. Brian had already climbed to camp 1 during my illness and had some advance acclimatization. It was evident as I huff through this labyrinth. Soon I come to a dead stop. Confronting me is a three foot crevasse with heavy flowing water which starts 10 feet down. I barely have time to consider this obstacle when I hear Brian shouting, "Wait till you get to this sucker!" I peer across my portion of the course to witness Brian atop something that looks really out of place. I rear back and jump this now seemingly insignificant chasm to witness how my partner will negotiate the "real" problem of the day.

My knees tremble at the sight of the challenge facing us. This contrivance is draped over a tunnel of smooth blue ice so perfectly polished no hand could have ever wrought such geometric perfection. Flowing through was water so cold and clear with the occasional chunks of jagged ice being the only hint of the speed with which that sluice would carry anything that fell victim to it. And here we are, standing one at a time six feet above the flow on four bamboo poles no thicker than four inches a piece. Lashed together with climbing rope from God knows when; none of the pieces are long enough to fully bridge the nine foot span. Anchoring them to the gravel which signifies the top of the glacier are bags of pebbles. From basecamp side the "bridge" slopes downhill significantly.

Brian's places one foot forward and then back. He then places the other foot forward and retreats back to the sacks of spilling gravel and stone. It is a death bridge hokey pokey that we both will play. Going downhill across this log flume with full 50 lb. backpacks is my introduction to K3. Danger lurks around every corner. Brian grabs the old climbing ropes attached to the ground. Pulling up on them means placing more force on the bamboo death bridge. Once committed, he sprints safely across. Then it is my turn.

Repeating the same motion, same dance, I employ a dishonorable alternative, sitting down and scooting across. If I was going to fall in, then my butt would be closer to the drink. I have the sense to disconnect all my pack straps just in case. Having made a few deep passages in the Southern Appalachian hills, I have learned to make crossings that way, lest the pack become an anchor. Brian laughs but I secretly know he wishes to have considered this. My "schooching" gets me downhill to the other, also leaking, bag of gravel. As I transition from that position to standing there is an uncertain moment. I maintain a grip on the rope and jerk myself and 50 lbs. clean up and over the adjacent buttress to which that portion of bamboo is attached. I am safely across and, like our bus ride through the Karakoram highway, spend the remainder of this climbing rotation with something else to dread upon our return.

Turns out our fears were more than justified. A very nice German woman named Dana, whom I was to meet higher on the mountain, lost her footing while crossing this bridge shortly after we met at camp 1. It was said that the backpack entangled her and she was swept immediately down the ice flu and disappeared from sight. She was irretrievably lodged underwater and beyond the assistance of her male companion. Rescuers spent five days trying to extricate the body from that underwater tomb. They used rope pulleys and had to chip away significant chunks of ice in a process that went on well beyond what they ever imagined. Each afternoon, the Pakistani rescuers would come to our mess tent and decry the difficulty of that chore. One of the guys had ice chunks in his hair. Part of me wanted to go down there and see this but a larger part of me did not. The rest of our team seems unaffected by this "anomaly". Ron and I are definitely keyed in.

It wasn't until one month after the expedition that Ron informed me that Afi, while returning to basecamp, also fell victim to that bridge of death. He apparently tumbled while climbing the uphill side from Broad Peak. According to Ron, Afi was able to use his ice axe to arrest himself and climb out before meeting the same fate as Dana. He came into basecamp dripping wet and close to hypothermic. I don't know exactly how far he was swept down that vortex into hell. Thank God he made it out of there. Considering what he had been doing up there at the time for his friends, it would have been a tragedy on top of tragedy.

SCALING THE WALL

Figure 26: Jugging up fixed lines to camp 1.
Photo John Quillen

Brian was down at the base of the mountain right below the fixed ropes where he had been patiently sitting on his pack and chewing on a power bar, for almost an hour. Between the bridge of death and this area was a significant climb over pure scree. That scree would give way with you at any time. I lost several minutes following the wrong trails and stepped up to my ankles more than once in mountain slough. I was huffing and puffing considerably. Brian asks if I have eaten anything. I lie. He knew I was lying.

"John, how do you expect to get up this mountain without any energy?"
He is right. With that I open one of the cheese and beef jerky packaged treats he threw me. I only eat the cheese. I mainly do that just to get him off my back, along with the pack I unceremoniously drop with a thud. This

is tough ground below a tough mountain. Broad Peak is letting me know that hiking up her skirt is going to take some courting.

As Brian disappears up the fixed lines, I wait, catching my breath and adjusting the harness. Stepping onto the soft snow on this cloudy morning with more precipitation spitting, I clip in with my safety line, then the jumar and began jugging up the fixed lines into seeming infinity. (A jumar, also known as an ascender, is a mechanical device that grips the rope in one direction. It has a handle and you attach webbing or perlon rope from it to your harness along with a backup safety line attached to a carabiner. The process of moving up on fixed lines is sometimes referred to as jugging.) I am prone to become lost in rhythmic activity like skinning up on skis or jugging a fixed line. The repetition of pushing the ascender up, switching anchors and repeating the entire process is comforting, like mowing or painting. The colossal effort of dragging your body and a fully laden pack up near vertical rock and ice is not. The lack of oxygen at now 16,000 feet combined with my prior debilitation makes for slow, heavily labored breathing, okay, gasping. I take four steps and stop for 30 breaths. Sometimes I can get to 10 steps and stop for 50 breaths.

This mathematical equation deviates according to the pitch. From my studies of Broad Peak on the internet, there were expectations of difficulty which have so far been wildly surpassed. Jugging up the fixed lines is difficult. Without fixed ropes, climbing this mountain would be all but impossible. It is that steep, relentless and sustained. A fall could be fatal. It is important to keep your head in the safety zone. I am fortunate in that no one is above or below me or this ascent to witness my belabored groans and oxygen deprived panting. There is no telling how many pitches I climb this day into our camp 1. I clip and unclip countless times. My lungs are on fire and I mentally remind myself to take deeper breaths instead of the short panting ones. Clouds move across the horizon that never seems to draw any nearer. I reach one particularly technical feature that ascends a cascading waterfall of snowmelt and is nearly vertical. It is like rock climbing with a safety back up. I flip the rope to see if it is free before clipping in. It scrapes across a very sharp rock overhang which imparts greater anxiety and sense of urgency about this section. I weight every rope fully before making any climb. If it holds me for a few seconds, I move as quickly as possible to the next piton. The high altitude porters who had fixed this rope suggested, after Ron remarked on the questionable condition of certain sections of fixed line, that we should, "..give it a little tug first". One section of a rope sheath has been wrapped with duct tape now loosened as the core is exposed. I see its innards from below with the weighting and slackening of this, my life line. I remind myself that a sheath is just that, outer protection.

From the initial clip until reaching our camp 1 is six hours. Combined with the walk over the scree and glacial field, I have eight and a half hours under my belt this particular day. Brian has been in camp 1 for quite a while. He is sitting there eating, of course. His ability to eat in all situations is key to his acclimatization success. That and Diamox. My only little helper is gingko biloba. On other expeditions it seemed to occasionally provide at least a psychological bump. It fails me miserably on this journey. I am fully out of breath and energy and collapse in the tent, crampons and all. It is a sight to which Brian is accustomed. Me being knackered on a climb and coming in late is an all too familiar sight with him. There are two Germans in tents adjacent to us on this little knob below the real camp 1. As a matter of fact, we are well below the proper camp 1 by a thousand feet, compliments of Aziz again. Brian whispers to me that the Germans were in our tents when he arrived. Apparently, he spared no niceties while evicting them. None of this was known to me as I cough my way headfirst into my new home and bid the Germans "Guten Abend". They just grumble and shuffle about in newly erected dwellings flanking our not so strategically placed ones.

As I lay there on this beautiful, windless evening, I forcefully ingest a cup of peanut butter and down some water. Too tired to start a stove, I collapse in my favorite piece of outdoor gear. It is the first time I get to use my sweetheart of a sleeping bag known collectively by all my friends as "Old Yeller". Old Yeller has been my most coveted possession since Denali. It is a 900 fill down bag that cost almost $650 US in 2006. You can bet that I have babied her since then in all ways, shapes and forms. I made a special hanger in my gear room reserved just for Old Yeller. They only made a 900 fill down for one year. Not only is it vintage, it is the warmest sleeping machine on the planet. It comes out in the Smoky Mountains about once per year when the temps are below zero. Any temperatures warmer than that and you will roast. I can't say enough about that sleeping bag. Climbing into her is like returning to the womb. It is a conveyance of magic and more comfortable than my bed at home.

It isn't long before Old Yeller draws me gently into a slumbering abyss. And sleep well I do, having been sufficiently sated and resting peacefully at 17,000 feet alongside our snoring German neighbors. Once again, these tents have been placed by our high altitude porter, Aziz. It is not something to which Brian and I are accustomed. We usually carry our own gear but this was part of the package and right now I wasn't arguing. Besides, we carried essentially everything else including stoves, fuel and food.

LIFE ALONG THE PARAPETS

17,500 feet July 2, 2013

The wind picks up during the night and next morning Ron and Scott were scheduled to join us at camp 2. I knew they would be early and begin packing up to move into Brian's cramped tent. Sure enough, by 9 a.m., Ron has radioed and is ascending the ropes into camp. This means that they left base camp around 5 a.m. Before long Scott is here. I begin making some breakfast in the cramped and now super cold conditions. It is snowing fairly heavily and the wind has become significant. Our group plan to climb up towards camp 2 is now in question as Ron dives into my former abode with Scott. We sit in for several hours this morning awaiting a break in the weather. These breaks typically happen before lunch as the sun rises in this part of the world before five a.m. Ron and Scott shuffle about, anxious to get moving on up the mountain. As usual, I am very content to sit idly melting copious amounts of snow for breakfast and coffee. I have recovered pretty well for my first trip up the mountain. I also figure that the sun will break through and blow out this gale before long so I lounge about as Brian and I trade elbows and knees in our cramped and wind-lashed quarters.

Sure enough it does clear by 11 a.m. and the rabbits are ready to run. We all suit up and began the ascent towards the "true" camp 1 and eventually camp 2. It takes me a full hour and a half just to reach the real camp 1 while Ron and Scott rocket up towards two. Brian and I call it quits at "true" camp 1. He had been there before. It is an honest climb on snow slopes to the crowded place I have seen only in pictures. Considering the ghetto of varying shades of fabric attached to one another precariously causes me to realize that I prefer our campsite and quickly retreat back there for another night. We rappel down in less than 30 minutes.

Scott and Ron come rolling in a few hours later. They don't actually reach camp 2 but probably get more than halfway. Now two to a tent, we all settle back into our camp for the evening. Rest is elusive as my body drifts downward into a corner forcing blood into my oxygen starved brain. The result is myriad dreamscapes of varying mountaineering tragedy combined with wind which rages throughout that evening. I am forced to continuously inhale a plate of tent nylon for hours. When the sun rises through the gale, I am up and shivering. I soon hear voices outside and poke my head into the nasty whiteness. It is Pouya, Aidin and Mojtaba with their million dollar smiles descending from camp 2. Aidin grabs my toboggan and we pretend to launch from the tent at them. Those boys are always having fun. I feel as if we were all now just one team forged from hardships on the journey.

Soon they drop down the fixed ropes and we begin melting snow and enjoying coffee. Brian and I make the tent quite jovial whilst Scott and Ron follow them down the hill. I was not keen to go out in this weather. Many other folks, however, were undeterred. Dropping from upper camps, they begin retreating to respective base camps in masse at the first sign of this change in weather. It is during this exodus that I meet the German woman, Dana climbing with one of the many international teams there. Our little perch is a good rest area before the last two thousand feet to the penitentes.

Descending in a white out is sufficiently challenging, rappelling on iced over ropes is more than exhilarating. Imagine dropping down a snow slope at your typical, self-controlled speed and then hitting a stretch where you slide about three times as fast until getting charge of the rope. I have a really good rappel device called the piranha that has added features for friction and performs quite well under these circumstances. It only takes about one hour to get to the scree slope that signifies the end of the route. Brian is there hiding some gear for next time. It is a good idea stolen from others. We stash our ice axes and various other things for the one-hour walk through the hell that is the icefall. (I place my ice axe in a slit between an ice boulder relatively unconcerned with the potential that the whole thing could collapse and permanently ensnare the tool).

Brian has a very quick pace and soon I lose him through what I come to call the "Labyrinth". The Labyrinth moves with the flowing glacier and there is always that hellish bridge with which to contend. Those ice ships and penitents really sail down the glacier several feet per day. It doesn't seem so bad going uphill on the bamboo bridge of death that is only 9 feet across. That bridge is not level and lists to one side. It probably still remains one of the most frightening things I have ever passed. One year ago, someone fell in and lost their life here. I don't know why they didn't bring an aluminum ladder for the span, last year, after someone fell in and lost their life.

Figure 27: Mazes of "ice ships" and penitentes complicate route finding.
Photo John Quillen

It takes me two hours to reach base camp. In essence, I get lost. Weaving through that hell of ice and scree, I get entombed in the catacomb of ice sculptures protruding like shark fins. You could enter one rabbit hole and ascend for five minutes only to be forced to turn around and enter another endless tunnel. Penitentes make for a penitentiary. Like a ship lost in a sea of confusion, I feel rudderless and adrift. I am incredibly frustrated and barely navigate my own ship into camp. In retrospect, the constant illness is taking its toll. Yes, I am over the stomach stuff at this point but at these elevations, full recovery is an elusive thing. I curse out loud and say things I wish that had not been uttered. Especially when I make a wrong turn that doubles my time into camp. Exhaustion and fatigue barely afford the energy to get back home. At one point I step through the ice and plunge up to my hip in water. Darkness isn't far from the horizon. I stumble over boulder after boulder until the safety of our mess tent comes into view behind furls of the Iranian flag. Pouya walks over and put his arms around me shouting, "John, John". Soon the other Iranians followed suit. This was our team and I was proud to regard them in that fashion. It feels like my family had been anticipating my return. Home means some rest time for which we were all definitely ready.

In base camp I also accidentally stumble into an argument between the Iranians and the Pakistani rope fixing mafia. I call them the mafia because they are extorting money ($300 US) from each climber for use of their ropes. I thought it a bit high but didn't complain, as it was part of the package for us. Ramin, by now solidly regarded as the Iranian leader, thinks the price high and refuses to pay. He offers to give them rope and equipment but the Pakistanis are interested in cash. Presumably, it is for a climbing school somewhere. Either way, if you pay that much there is an expectation of service. Those ropes and that bridge are definitely a disservice, as events would later prove.

I sit in the mess tent drinking tea, too exhausted to even remove my harness listening to the back and forth between Ramin and the Pakistanis. Ramin is resolute and the HAP isn't budging. It is a Mexican standoff and the Pakistani blinks. The remainder of the Iranians are unified behind their leader. The end result is a request by the Pakistani that they not use their ropes. He essentially has no other choice. I liken it to the request of Brian asking the Germans to vacate our tents. Which they did, until we left.

I am approached by our liaison officer. He is saying goodbye and leaving the expedition. His liaison officer buddy from another expedition is having trouble acclimatizing and Yawer plans to accompany him off the glacier. His parting words are of great comfort. "The road to Islamabad is closed, all trekkers are being flown out of Skardu as a result of the incident at Nanga Parbat." It is the best present I have received on the trip. True or not, the anxiety of facing that 30-hour ride is neutralized. We embrace and he departs.

Princes of Camelot

4:45 a.m.: I am awakened by unadulterated rays of sun absent from our mountain for several days. This glorious morning is heralded by the singing of none other than Mojtaba. He is so happy to see the sun that he is serenading the event and the promise of a beautiful day. In his late twenties, Mojtaba is full of life and energy. He is always smiling, laughing and consistently animated. I rate his English skills as minimal but communication is no problem. He seems to learn more English as a result of our interactions as the expedition progresses. My Farsi doesn't fare so well. Mojtaba discussed his profession as a firefighter in Tehran. I soon learn that he is engaged to be married in September. Brian and I tease him about that. Brian cites me as an example of the loneliness of old age and I refer to Brian as a textbook example of hen pecked-ness. Mojtaba clearly understands both our motives and laughs with us as we needle him and each other.

Figure 28: Mojtaba Jarahi with Ramin.
Photo John Quillen

71

Always dangling from his neck is a leather pouch given to him by his girlfriend. When I inquire about it, he removes the tiny container and unsnaps the enclosure to produce a miniature version of the Koran that he proudly hands to me. I thumb through the document so small you can barely open it. I had a similar version of the King James Bible somewhere back at my house in Knoxville. Mojtaba is a devout Muslim who prays openly. I remember seeing him at one of the roadside mosques at which we had stopped along the way bowing down and offering prayers. Many of the Iranians exercised their religious beliefs in that fashion but never pushed it upon us or in any way derided our Christian faith. I remember one conversation during which he asked our religious beliefs and we told him and he smiled and nodded towards us. We were just a group of mountaineers in a tent sharing our lives and culture. I would have to say that was a highlight of the trip for me.

Brian and I had work to do this day, though. When the sun shines on expedition you do one of three things, climb, laundry or shower. Since it is a planned rest day, laundry is first on the list. Having secured a bucket and gallon of hot water we are off to the races. Those filthy socks, underwear and shirts are getting a thorough scrubbing compliments of the dishwashing soap procured in Skardu. The dishwashing soap suds up great and we take turns scrubbing and rinsing the pile, then hanging it up on an improvised close-line between our tents. This seemingly mundane chore confers great joy on this outstanding day. I am soon ready for a shower which is performed in a similar fashion and a shave. For that, I was conscripted by another one of the Iranians, Afshin. He takes me to a rock and begins clipping my errant beard with a pair of hand clippers as if I were a sheep in need of shearing. Afi spends a full 30 minutes bush hogging the underbrush that has become my face. This act underscores the character of the Iranians. When something needs doing, they rise to meet the task no matter how unpleasant. When he is finished I march into the dining tent whereupon Ramin and Azim begin applauding. I look into a mirror and realize they have just made me an Iranian. Afi's barbering confers upon me a look which is a cross between Mojtaba and Ramin.

Figure 29: The author receives a shave, compliments of Afshin.
Photo Scott Powrie

It is such a great day that I actually make a list of all the things for which I am thankful at that point. It is an A plus day on the mountain. We are clean, rested, well fed and ready to climb some more. I am not vomiting or suffering from any physical malady. I do make a note in my journal that reads as follows: "On a physical level, this is the most difficult thing I have ever done." In my appreciation list there is an asterisk beside the word K2. She is reigning in all her glory this day and I take copious pictures and video. To sleep beneath this giant is a privilege. My fingernails are cracking, though. Strange phenomena to see them break by looking at them too intently. It appears as if I have been clawing my way out of a stone cage.

Rumblings From the Dragon's Lair

July 3, 2013

Our next foray up the hill is on a good weather day. After a relaxing breakfast, Brian and I set a leisurely pace to camp 1. I am able to negotiate the Labyrinth with more dexterity and confidence this time, reducing my time to the start of the fixed ropes to one and a half hours. The hazardous bridge crossing is still just that, hazardous and frightening. I reach the fixed rope and began jugging. Halfway up Brian radios me to check on my status. Brian is always checking in on me and there is no better guy to have watching your back on strange turf. I reply something cocky and totally smart. This lets him know that he needn't anticipate another lifeless, half dead companion who couldn't melt his own snow. Although breathing is still labored, I cut two hours off my time and come rolling into camp 1 feeling like a true champion. Brian has been there for a while and is happy to see me in high spirits instead of totally demoralized. I believe that my time to camp 1 from base camp is about five hours.

Figure 30: Author suits up for another rotation to upper camps.
Photo Scott Powrie

That evening we bask in the fading Karakoram sunset from our camp 1 as a noise from the west shoulder of Broad Peak brings our attention to a rumbling from the bowels of this mountain. A dragon is emerging from within K3. As it stirs, 100 yards of snow cleave as if shaven by a royal barber. The result is an avalanche parallel to our campsite that brings a cascading wave of white-capping snow beyond our line of sight. It follows a line directly down the path that a German group had been ascending earlier in the day. Were anyone off the fixed lines climbing as they were, they would perish. But no one is. These avalanches are a constant reminder of the seriousness of this endeavor. Even from base camp, we were awakened more than once by the sounds like atomic bombs reigning spindrift down into the Labyrinth.

The next morning we suit up and begin our climb to camp 2. Since we had climbed to the true camp 1, that portion is a relative piece of cake. The way it works in the acclimatization game, however, is thus: You perform well to the point of your last height. Then comes the brick wall. For me that point is true camp 1. Brian disappears into the heavens as I scramble across the scree onto the fixed ropes above the tent city at the "true" camp 1. The weather is ideal for this kind of day. It is sunny but cool and crisp, a definite Chap Stick and sunblock kind of climbing event.

I encounter quite a logjam on the fixed ropes as folks are descending from summit pushes. In all, only one of the dozens had made the top. (Broad Peak was to allow only eight summits this year and claim the lives of five who succeed) The descending mountaineers cause me to wait at anchor points as they rappel by. These men are ready to get the heck back to base camp. I pass people with whom I had gotten to know while climbing this hill, all Germans. They are very nice and probably look to occupy our now empty tents at lower camp 1. People always ask from where we hail. The Europeans would give me a fist bump as they pass when I say "US." It must mean they think we are brave for being here. (We were just a couple of the very few Americans in the Karakoram region) There are Sherpa climbing the hill and their prowess never fails to impress. If ever a creature were made for the heights twas their ilk. I presume they are employed by the guided groups such as Amical etc. Brian later informs me that he got to know one of them who lost a cousin nearby in the Nanga Parbat massacre. *"I'm never coming back to this f***ing hellhole."* He tells my partner. Uncharacteristic rumblings from a race known for their peaceful nature. The Nanga Parbat incident touched many to their core. You expect the avalanches on expedition but not mass murder.

After the logjam I continue jugging and jugging and jugging. Gaining altitude to almost 19,000 feet, I start coughing up weird things like my lungs. I won't go into details but if my good friend and climbing partner Dr. Dan Walters were there he would probably have told me to descend. At one point I cough up some bloody phlegm and frighten myself into a mini panic. I needed to take some breaths and drink more water. Reaching for the holster I lift a bottle with few sips remaining. It is the most difficult part of this climb for me and it never, ever seems to relent. Ten hours after I leave camp 1, I am still ascending with no relief in sight. It is pitch after pitch after pitch of fixed rope. Scott and Ron warned me of this merciless ascent and they did not under report. When I finally roll into this hillside full of scree with tents, the day is nearly night. I am more tired, exhausted and dehydrated than at any point I can ever remember in my life. I have absolutely zero gas left in the tank. I uncertain as to whether or not I can make it to my tent, provided I knew which tent it could be. There are quite a few nylon skeletons on this hillside ghost town and if it is one at the upper reaches of the hill, I don't think I can make it, seriously.

I spy the Eureka tents we had inspected back in Skardu and one is sitting on something, half hanging off the mountain. I disconnect from the last section of fixed rope wishing that there were more leading to the upper tents. As I pick my way towards them, ice axe in hand, a voice summons me from one of the lower tents. It is Azim, the Iranian "Silver Fox". It is like fumbling through a faraway castle full of empty chambers and having a member of your family emerge from a closed room smiling. He is motioning me to him to come in. I greet him and almost collapse. Azim could tell how tired I was and, in his limited English, (through hand gestures I surmise) offers to cook me dinner. I love that man. Typical Iranian hospitality at 20,000 feet. What I need, however, is water and he has precious little so I move on. How that "Silver Fox" could get to camp 2 so much ahead of us is testament to his character and ability. You see, Azim was a political prisoner in Iran for many years on multiple occasions. As we spoke through the translation of Ramin, I learned that he stood for his beliefs in defiance of the Iranian government to the point of going to prison, three times! He climbs solo and covers large distances. Azim has been alone at camp 2 for an undetermined amount of time, not counting the hours Brian has preceded me.

Figure 31: Broad Peak Camp 2, 20,300 feet.
Photo Scott Powrie

I pick my way to this half dome that is humpbacked, hanging off a cliff and sidling. Since no one else is in camp besides the two of us and Azim, I can have this tent to myself. It is no great benefit and in retrospect I would have been much better off with Brian. Brian snagged the better spot and I don't blame him. I bargain with him to trade some beef jerky for a quart of water as I lean over to enter the vestibule of a neighboring abode. My boots seem permanent attachments to my feet and the effort to remove them seems equal to the ascent. Collapsing half in and half out, I start begging Brian for water. I tear open some homemade beef jerky produced especially for us from my friend, Mike McMurray and sip from a quart of water as I listen to the approaching windstorm that rolls in pushing the sun away, threatening to blow us off this mountain.

Forced to converse through hand held radios, we are adjacent but unable to shout to each other. I had seen wind like this in the mountains before only once, and that was on Huascaran in Peru. This night proves eventful and somewhat uneasy. Can I blow off the mountain? It has happened. Thank goodness it did not. I lay motionless inside "Old Yeller" and once again, fall ready victim to her mystic trance. My exhaustion trumps most all concern and I am out before long only to awaken multiple times to the seeming sound of freight trains converging in all directions. On top of that is random thunder interspersed amidst the howling winds. What unfolds is a battle between exhaustion and fear. Fortunately, exhaustion prevails and Old Yeller keeps me safe throughout what will prove to be our final night on the heights.

Morning comes, as it usually does in the Karakoram, at 4.45 a.m. We awake and start radioing each other, lazy as that sounds. However, we can't breach the still full on gale. In fact, it seems as if the wind has increased with the advent of the day's first light. Two hours later, we are debating a plan of action. Originally we were to make a climb towards camp 3 then drop all the way down to base camp for a long rest before coming back for the summit or a final acclimatization run contingent upon our assessment at base camp. Now it is looking as if we might have to stay here another night. However, by 10 a.m., as if on cue, the wind dies, the sun pops out and Brian is heading up to camp 3.

Figure 32: On the rope above camp 2
Photo Brian Moran

His climb is short lived. Within 45 minutes he has had enough and exhibits a readiness to drop back to base camp. Teasing him about his most valiant and lengthy efforts, Brian unclips from the fixed line as I peer through the vestibule of my tent to video and verbally taunt him. I enjoy the rest as I make coffee, oatmeal and pack up Old Yeller. I wanted to put Old Yeller in the waterproof bag to protect her and create some weight in this tent. I also added a bunch of good-sized rocks on the front and back inside of the tent just in case. The next time I arrive here, Old Yeller and my extra clothes, hand warmers, food and fuel will be ready for a summit bid. Things seem to finally be lining up.

There is another video of Brian beginning his descent from camp 2 to base camp. I later notice the dialogue between us at this time. He begins rappelling and I ask him to weight the anchor to make sure. Brian says, *"I'll see you at camp 1."*

For some reason beyond my comprehension, in what proves to be a spate of prophetic utterances I reply, *"I'll see you before then."*

SLAPPED BY THE BEAST'S TAIL

As we rappel down from the camp, I snap photos of K2 from this height. It is turning into a very nice, crisp day as the sun chases many of the clouds back into China. K2 never ceases to impress me. I anticipate blowing these pictures up for those bare walls of my home. Since it is such a nice day, I avail myself of many similar photo ops down the line. Brian descends about one rope pitch ahead at all times. After all the time in country, I was reaching my stride. Having decided to down some coffee and oatmeal turns out to be one of the best decisions of the expedition. I resist the temptation to just go straight to base camp with no sustenance. All this was done during Brian's short jaunt towards camp 3. Azim, however, flies straight on to camp 3 and spends the night. Those Iranians are amazing. He is to join Pouya, Mojtaba, Aidin and Afi who are already there.

Figure 33: The Author rappels down from camp 2
Photo Brian Moran

But not me. It is base camp and thicker airtime. Same for Brian. As we descend into camp 1, the real camp 1, I transition back onto the scree that serves as tent platforms for the majority of Broad Peak climbers. Our camp 1 is lower because that is where our high altitude porter, Aziz, lazily established the camp. It ends up being a good thing for me because it deducts an hour from total climbing time. I watch Brian disappear back onto the snow and the fixed lines. I also run into a German that I have gotten to know through our rotations on the mountain. He is one of the snoring dudes next to us that first night who thought they would occupy our tents before Brian ejected them. It is, apparently, a European thing to occupy an unoccupied tent, as we later learned. (*This happened as I was relating the story over dinner at basecamp to the Iranians. I noticed the absence of concern on Ramin's face as Brian and I ranted about the incursion. Later on he confessed that they all routinely did the same thing higher up.*) Ownership is relative to necessity. After exchanging pleasantries with the German I step back onto the snow and fixed line below real camp 1. Very few minutes pass before I arrive at the next anchor.

There is a bit of gap between pitons at this particular anchor spot which means that in order to transition you must first leave your safety line on the upper rope while pulling the lower rope for enough of a byte to clip through your descending device or figure 8. It requires a bit of maneuvering. (*By this point in the descent, we have probably made close to 80 of these.*) As some might say, *"It was a stretch."* It was tempting to simply forgo the safety and take a step between the anchors. This shelf was somewhat tricky and I consider doing that very thing for a second. The snow is so firmly packed at this spot that even with crampons, I envision careening undeterred three thousand feet onto the Godwin-Austin glacier, which prompts me to abandon that careless scheme. As I grab the downward line it is taught. In my head this signifies someone ascending and implies a considerable wait time. I clip my ascender into the lower line so I can look around the massive rock outcropping to see which German is coming up. What I spy from the corner of this massive boulder as I crane my neck awkwardly is most unexpected. One hundred feet below lies my partner face down in the snow.

WATERLOO

I have climbed enough with Brian to know that he never takes those kinds of breaks. Me, on the other hand, quite a few. It is not uncommon to see me totally prone or bent over my ice axe. I probably look dead most of the time on the mountain because breathing is such a chore for my genetically challenged lungs. Unlike renowned alpinist Ed Viesturs, who has been measured to have significantly increased lung capacity I have no doubt that mine is significantly reduced and would likely be told to take up another hobby such as no altitude oxygen breathing.

I shout down to him, *"Brian, Brian, what is happening?"*
His response is quick, *"I think my leg is broken!"*

Knowing Brian wouldn't joke about such a thing, I quickly realize that he likely had accurately assessed his injury fifteen minutes earlier as I was socializing with the German. I fumble for a second trying to clip into the taught line. So many thoughts are running through my head that I can't focus on getting down to him. What does this mean? How bad off is he, How am I to get him down? I quickly snap to, wrangle enough rope to jam through my figure 8 and began my rappel 90 feet down to a point just above where he is laying prone on the 45-degree snow slope. I almost hesitate because I lack a good plan in my head as I drop down into the ocean of white and the snow pillow upon which my partner lay. There on this beautiful, crisp afternoon at 18,000 feet, one thousand feet above our camp 1, Brian is in trouble. And we are alone.

My first task is to secure him to the fixed rope. It is apparent that this malady occurred independent of the static line to which I am now permanently securing us both. Next task is to splint his leg. It occurs to me that an ice axe is the right shape to fit against the inside of his leg and brace the foot. A trekking pole will have to do for the other side. We carry extra webbing for rescue situations. The end result of this webbing and ice axe machination is some form of modern art. It isn't pretty and I'm not the lightest touch. For all I know, he has a bone sticking out. The way I make him yell drives that home. It doesn't matter. My primary purpose is to get him to that little speck at the bottom of the slope which I only know from memory is our set of tents. If he slips off this rope to either side, it will be a terminal slide with permanent consequences. I was starting to appreciate my laziness earlier in the day opting to drink coffee and eat oatmeal. It was all that was on my stomach for the past day. The Godwin-Austin glacier was 2500 feet below and stretches like a highway for dozens of miles. On the far right of our field of view is a place, obscured by clouds that we know to be base camp. Between us and that landform is the Labyrinth and Bridge of Death. Before ever considering these hazards, we have to reach our camp 1. From that point down is the steepest portion of climbing thus far on Broad Peak.

Weather is good but it was now after noon. Cognizant of the race against time, I know if he can be dropped to the tent at camp 1, we can wait until morning for someone to come up from base camp. Presently, however, Brian is getting cold and makes mention of the possibility of going into shock. New cloud forms rollover from K2 suggesting a change in weather. I really get serious at this point. Attaching my ascending device above me on the rope to keep us both from slipping down either side from which we had witnessed the avalanches earlier, I remove his closed cell foam sleeping pad and tie it around him. This will provide a sled so he can drop with minimal friction down the late afternoon, warm, and sticky snow. Brian is clipped into the rope and I run a carabiner through the back of his harness. I can now run the remaining fixed rope through my figure 8 descender and lower him, slowly, down the line. Every five feet, I have to stop and lower my ascender. It is laborious and slow. We make progress but it is insufficient.

Brian is getting cold due to lying on the snow and his hands and his pants are wet. I fish deep into my pack to produce a pair of down mittens for him. I've not paid much attention to my leather gloves that were also completely soaked. Since I am actively moving, however, cold isn't much of a concern for me although I am hyper cognizant of my susceptibility to frostbite. He knows to drink water and we finish both our bottles in short order. This lowering and dropping the ascender is fairly inefficient but I can concoct no other way to keep us both from tobogganing past the only flat spot which is in our crosshairs.

Brian reminds me that we are scheduled for a radio check in call to base camp at four p.m. It is now three o'clock and this process has been underway for about two hours. I turn on the radio and make a call just in case. There is no response. We continue with the descent. When I lower Brian, it is inevitably jerky as a result of the snow friction and causes considerable pain in my climbing partner. There is little I can do. Brian is quite courageous and does not complain, although I hear a few distinct grunts when I am a little quick with the rope.

We are both tiring of this process and I am running out of steam. It has now been a full three hours since I first reached Brian. Almost as if from the heavens, a figure appears at the top of the fixed rope. I first think it is Ramin but soon realize it is Mojtaba descending from camp 3. I frantically motion him down and enlist his support. Mojtaba was a paramedic and firefighter in Tehran. At 28 years old he has considerable mountain experience. Mojtaba is one of what Brian and I called the "three young bucks." Those three bucks are undoubtedly the strongest, boldest climbers in our expedition. There was little doubt they would lead the summit assault on the new Broad Peak route. It is a project upon which the Iranian team has concentrated since their last attempt in 2009. Putting a new route on an 8000-meter peak is a huge deal in the world of climbing. It is well publicized and researched. Now, after a rotation to camp 3, the Iranians are fully in position to mount a serious summit bid.

Mojtaba quickly rappels to my position in his usually animated state, full of smiles. It doesn't take long for him to understand that we have a real situation here and he is immediately drafted into service. We change our lowering system as a result of the extra set of hands. I now have Mojtaba short rope Brian from the bottom and I remove the ascender. There is a language gap that never seems so wide as at this present moment. Mojtaba defers to me and my scheme. It speeds up the lowering dramatically. Mojtaba is now pulling Brian as I let down rope. Those little tent specs are finally getting bigger. I also am getting close enough to our camp 1 to see a couple of folks down there. I holler for them to come and assist. Without fail, one of the climbers begins ascending in our direction. It is some Germans and their kindness will become integral to this rescue. To give you an idea of what it means to ascend to our position consider this. They have just climbed over four hours of near vertical rock and snow and ice to reach this point. Before they barely have time to lay down their packs they are enlisted to assist in a rescue that involves another stretch of climbing. Without hesitation, one of them suits back up and resumes climbing yet again. He is able to reach us within an hour as we were shortening the distance considerably at this point. Immediately I task him with command of Brian's backpack. Mojtaba has been shouldering it along with his own pack and short roping Brian the whole time. It underscores the strength and fearlessness of this young man.

Figure 34: Mojtaba guides injured Brian as I let out rope. Our camp 1 is the flat spot directly below.
Photo John Quillen

Four o'clock comes and I make the scheduled radio call to base camp. Scott is on the line when I deliver the news. He springs into action and what ensues are a score of subsequent radio transmissions. Ron contacts Concordia where a team of high altitude porters (HAPs) that happened to have rescue training are assembled and on their way. We continue lowering Brian until the scree line of camp 1. I know that he is in tremendous pain but keep telling myself it has to be less serious than we imagine. Soon we enlist the two Germans who each grab a limb. We carry him to one of our tents that is fortunately unoccupied by other Germans. It is at this point that Mojtaba descends to base camp. He is dog-tired and hasn't planned on this big detour. I insist that he go down since we know the HAPs are on the way up along with Ron and Brian and Aziz, our own HAP. I literally have to push Mojtaba down the hill. There is no point in both of us descending in the dark.

I have some time in the fading daylight to lay Brian down and begin removing his wet clothes. We leave his boots on to keep any swelling in check. He has a down suit that works perfectly for what is surely to become a vertical descent. I put him in a sleeping bag, give him some water and check on the progress of the HAPs. Much to our relief, they are making record time. Brian is bearing up well and happy to be in the tent. Neither of us can imagine what the remainder of his descent will entail. We are just thrilled to be resting for a bit. I thank the Germans and take them up on their offer to use their collected snow. It saves me additional effort as I pull up a rock next to Brian's tent and begin making water. I haven't had much to drink since that morning. My quart was gone hours ago.

We don't have to wait long. Aziz is first up the rope and is immediately followed by five Pakistani HAPs. How they cover that distance in such short order is nothing less than miraculous. They go quickly to work putting bamboo splints and removing my temporary mess from Brian's busted leg. These guys are the Pakistani version of Sherpa. They perform like animals at elevation and remain acclimatized throughout the climbing season. They have him wrapped up in a blue plastic children's sled and are descending down the fixed ropes in lightning speed with my buddy on a toboggan ride he shall never forget. It has to be close to six p.m. at this point. Ron radios to let me know he is three pitches from camp and I tell him to stay put, that I am resting for a minute and beginning the remainder of my descent. He agrees to wait for me there. I gather my kit from this camp, check both tents for remaining gear and start rappelling down the line. It is dark now and my headlamp is doing its job. The brief rest gives me sufficient energy to complete this descent. I come to one pitch above Ron and the HAPs with Brian. He advises me via radio to wait until the line is clear. I then descended to Ron and we leapfrog down the hill. I see very little of Brian and the rescue crew from that point. They lower him down faster than I can rappel. It is both amazing and fearful.

Figure 35: High Altitude Porters tend to Brian's leg at camp 1.
Photo John Quillen

When I finally reach Ron on the fixed rope, we continue the descent and he disappears into the night. I am now alone on Broad Peak with about 500 feet to go and it is peaceful and comforting to know that Brian is in good hands. When I reach the scree signifying the end out the route, someone is there with a light to point my way down the nearly invisible path. I first think it to be Ron but judging by the darkness and height of the individual realize it is not. I say, *"Good to have someone here with the light!"* Since his headlamp is staring me in the face I can't tell and really don't care whom it may be. I assume it is one of the HAPs. It takes me a minute to remove my crampons and get squared away. In five minutes time this nameless individual guides me down that detritus pathway of gravel. There is one spot that I almost overlook into which I most definitely would have stepped into a crack had it not been for the light of this dark figure who turns around and illuminates this four foot gap between mountain and the Labyrinth. Soon afterward he disappears gently into the darkness. I try to follow him through the scree but then realize how exhausted I have become. I am stumbling and getting off route and my mystery guide is long gone. I spy a headlamp one hundred yards ahead and below. I resolve to catch up to that HAP and not lose him this time.

Within a few minutes I do catch up and shout something in his direction. It was some sort of thank you. However, I soon discover that I am thanking Ron who has no idea of what I am speaking. He has seen no HAPs between the two of us and dismisses it as an altitude hallucination. I begin to do the same since there is no way anyone could have slipped away between us. I can assure you that a person was there waiting for me that never spoke a word. He just stood with his headlamp pointing to my feet so I could remove the crampons. I was not surprised that a porter would do such a thing. Such is the nature of the Pakistani people. For all I knew he was one of the rescue group. The thought did not occur to me that I may have met my guardian angel until much later.

I stumble through the Labyrinth in the dark. Ron is on point and I make sure not to lose him. His route finding is meticulous. Ron has an aptitude for altitude and climbing plus a body to perform in his fifties. He voices concern about the bridge crossing which ignites my latent and all but forgotten terror of that task. We have by now been informed that the German woman I had met on our first rotation had fallen off this death trap and come to rest a quarter mile down the ice flu where she was lodged until drowning. Her body lay there for days before a rescue team could extricate her. This mountain was claiming victims at an alarming rate for the year.

When we reach the bamboo bridge both Ron and I cross very carefully and with no problems. Darkness is like blinders on the horse. This includes the crevasse jumping that immediately follows. I can only imagine how they got Brian through here. I knew the German lady was on his mind as well. Either way, we weave our way through the Labyrinth with Ron's guidance and soon find ourselves chasing a cadre of headlamps nearing the hill that separates this minefield from our base camp. I'm taken back to the time, in the daylight, when I could hardly complete the chore. As we pick our way through boulders and chaff I come upon two guys holding Brian. It is the first time that I have seen him since camp 1 some four hours ago. Milling about boulders a group of 15 men converse in Urdu about how to get Brian across the last river of ice. I inquire about his shape and Brian holds a stiff upper lip while indicating that he is in good hands. At the same time I am approached by another mysterious, dark figure who tries to grab my backpack. It is none other than Mojtaba and he doesn't take no for an answer. I am too tired to argue. We join Brian for his final few yards into base camp. Muhammad Ali, assistant cook, proudly carries him on his back for the last feet of the ascent. Brian is now safely off the flanks of Broad Peak.

KNIGHTS ERRANT: BRIAN'S GUARDIAN ANGELS

Someone had enlisted the services of a German doctor from another expedition. Surreptitiously, he happens to be an orthopedic specialist. This physician has us lay Brian on the floor of the dining tent as we cut away clothing and remove his boots. It is very late in the evening and a curious crowd has assembled from other base camps. I have to push my way through the mix to get next to my buddy. He is going to need some support because this medicine man has me prep him for a shot. Brian is in agony and holding back what must be excruciating pain. Several of us grab limbs and I pump Brian's arm for the approaching needle. When I ask the physician about the medication he indicates it is ketamine. Brian is soon slipping into a drug induced trip and squeezes our hands until I think he will break my bones. Everyone chuckles as Brian wails, *"Don't let me off the rope, John, keep that rope tight!"* Mentally, Brian is back on the snowfield above camp 1 as the ketamine courses through his veins. The doctor then sets and splints his leg with bits of closed cell foam and gauze. The facility with which he operates is very impressive. The result is more than a makeshift job of casting.

By one a.m. the doctoring is complete and crowd dissipates. I bring my sleeping kit from the tent to be with him lest he need something. Sure enough, by three a.m., the medication has worn off and he is writhing in pain. Brian begs me to find some medication but I dare not wake anyone at this hour. Leaving the dining tent, I pace about our compound hoping for someone to assist me. Ron is stirring from his tent and I quickly run over there in the darkness and cold of this early hour. We put Brian off until 5.30 a.m. at which time Ron escorts me over to the German basecamp.

Figure 36: Brian puts a good face on a bad situation
Photo Scott Powrie

The only people awake at the German camp are the cook staff and when I ask for the "doctors" tent, they point in the direction of what we presume is the orthopedic specialists domicile. Ron and I sheepishly approach the sleeping inhabitant. "Excuse me," Ron politely murmurs. We soon hear some stirring and unzipping. Seconds later the outer vestibule is opening to reveal the face of someone totally unfamiliar. It is obvious we have been sent to the wrong tent. Turns out we have been directed to the residence of another physician who, without blinking an eye and with perfect English, so kindly produces a blister pack of morphine and detailed dosage instructions for Brian. He is a colleague of the other doctor (whose name we never recorded) and has been briefed, apparently, on the situation. His generosity for someone he has never met is overwhelming. This doctor, Christian Buchsteiner, comes to visit Brian later in the morning along with another German that specializes in high altitude medicine. That physician administers heparin shots to Brian's stomach to prevent blood clots due to this high altitude. Inactivity will make him susceptible to that particular malady. In all Brian acknowledges his extreme luck to have the attention available. The German physicians graciously donate their time and talents to setting his leg, fabricating a temporary cast and making him comfortable. This includes checking on him daily as we await helicopter evacuation. I secretly wonder if any of those guys had been evicted from our tents by Brian earlier on but resist the urge to plant that seed in Brian's head.

As he lay in the mess tent where we can tend to him unobstructed, Scott contacts Global Rescue to dispatch a helicopter. We had all purchased rescue insurance as recommended by our ground agents. Global Rescue is tasked with the responsibility of arranging evacuation via the Pakistani military. In this zone, the military is the only entity allowed to execute rescue unlike in the Himalaya proper where commercial operations are very quick to respond. On that first day, clouds and snow squalls ground our exit plan. It signifies a spell of ugly weather and snow for many days. Accumulating through the nights, deposits of up to four inches at times fall on our base camp. That, combined with winds and low visibility prohibit any rescue for six days. Six days of anxious waiting, satellite phone calls and broken dispatches are creating great concern for Brian's condition.

Via the contacts we are able to make, the notion of evacuating Brian with porters or donkeys is suggested. This comes from the triage specialist at Global Rescue. I intervene to nix these schemes immediately. We can barely move Brian in his present state and further jarring would only exacerbate his condition. By day four all of our medical support has packed up and trekked down the Baltoro glacier headed for Germany. Hope is dimming. The inevitable doubting leads to speculation about whether or not the helicopters are just a pipe dream. Dutifully each morning I awake at sunrise and pack my sleeping bag, roll up the inflatable pad and carry my pack to the dining tent in preparation for a hasty departure that is not to be. Pakistan is feeling like a prison from which there is no escape. I can unzip a vestibule and rip three quarters of a nail clean off. My fingernails are now considerably more jagged and torn in strange patterns that resemble the rugged Karakoram skyline.

Figure 37: Dark days of weather and waiting in basecamp.
Photo Scott Powrie

Down time is spent in the mess tent with all team members now waiting out this spate of nasty weather. I rarely remove my puffy down parka for a week. I remember the look on Mojtaba's comrades faces as they trickle into the mess tent the following morning and see Brian sprawled out with his leg splinted and covered with sleeping bags. The Iranians play games, produce copious foods from their barrels and laugh. They raise our spirits and help tend to Brian. I am fired from that duty due to my lack of delicate touch. It is suggested there was no need for dentistry. Scott and Aidin could gently lift his leg while the bandages are removed for temporary relief. I'm only allowed to reposition sleeping bags and makeshift pillows.

He does so kindly allow me attend to his bodily functions, though. One story involves the time when I clear the tent to afford Brian some privacy following breakfast and coffee. Having produced a bucket lined with a trash bag, I am now standing guard at the main entrance. Muhammid Ali passes by in the cold, foggy haze of a socked in morning. He stops mid stride to ascertain the purpose of my curious, guard like position. Muhammid knows as much English as I know Urdu. He says, "*Brian*" and points in the tent. I make a universal gesture that indicates what he was doing in there. As I make the gesture, Muhammid starts laughing, which has the effect of making me laugh. Soon we are both laughing uncontrollably at the thought of how he must be attending to this function in his condition. Brian hears our laughter and shouts,

'*What's going on out there?*'

I reply, "*Muhammid Ali is here and I told him what you are doing and he got me laughing.*"

Still standing there, Muhammid starts laughing again, which results in me laughing again and Brian is shouting at us because it is interrupting his routine in there. We continue to giggle like school girls. We attempt to restrain ourselves out of respect for Brian but about that time, Ganga approaches the tent. Her English is about like Muhammid's. Brian hears Ganga outside and says, "*What are you doing, holding a party out there making fun of me?*" It was quite funny having to hand gesture to Ganga what was happening in the place where she took all of her meals.

We really get to know our team mates during this period and I relish the sharing of our cultures. I tease Aidin quite a bit because his last name is on one of the barrels facing my tent. Every time I see him I say, "*Hey, Aidin Bozorgi.*" Just to mess with him. He knows my game is to get him to ask me how I came to know his last name and refuses to fall for the ploy. He always looks at me with that toothy smile and proceeds unfettered. All three of the "young bucks" become like little brothers to Brian, Scott and myself. Their good nature and joviality makes them always the center of attention amongst our group. Pouya speaks no English but you know he is a good guy because of what he does. He is always offering to help you do, complete or pass something. We are also visited once again by Marty Schmidt and his son, Denali.

THE ROYAL SUCCESSION, LIKE FATHER LIKE SON

Marty Schmidt was fresh off his most recent Everest trip where he successfully guided clients for an untold number of years. It was a vocation that took him to the summit of many of the 14 highest peaks in the world and kept him travelling constantly between his home in New Zealand and the high mountain ranges. Listening to him speak of these conquests I soon realized he never tired of them.

Marty was visiting our basecamp early in the expedition and introduced himself, his son, Denali and team mate Chris Warner. Naming your son after a mountain can carry inherent risks; I was reminded of Willi Unsoeld's daughter, Devi. Unsoeld, arguably one of the boldest mountaineers the US ever produced, was one of Everest's first summiters. He and partner, Tom Hornbein picked their way along the technically challenging West ridge just days after Jim Whittaker planted an American flag on top in 1963. It was probably the greatest and arguably last "true ascent" of that peak. Both men paid with lost digits and suffered a horrible bivouac at 28,000 feet. To this day it is an unrepeated feat.

Unsoeld chose the name of a beautiful peak called Nanda Devi in the Hindu Kush range, alleged dwelling place of Hindu Gods, for his daughter. Naturally, Devi Unsoeld was mystically drawn to her namesake peak. She was quoted as saying, "...*There is something within me about this mountain ever since I was born.*" It was there, along with her Father and other members of the last expedition allowed to climb that peak, that she began experiencing stomach problems at a high camp and died on July 10, 1976. It was said that Unsoeld's hair turned white overnight as a result. I often wondered how he ever faced his wife in light of that circumstance.

As I shook hands with Denali he grasped me firmly and looked directly into my eyes. At 26 years old this mountaineer followed in his legendary

Father's tracks up many peaks. He and friend Chris Warner got along famously with the Iranians who were the same age and had similar climbing ambitions. The Schmidt's plan to scale Broad Peak and then ultimately move over to K2 was equally bold, though not unheard of. One of our own expedition members, Ganga, was following the same plan.

Bad weather during the expedition would find Marty and Denali back in our mess tent waiting out storm days. We had a couple of nasty spells. They were characterized by wind and overnight snow squalls of three to four inches. I remember waking up to what I thought would be bright days as the darkness was chased from inside my tent, only to find it an illusion peering out to bright whiteness. The sun toyed with us. Many mornings would see breakfast fading imperceptibly into lunch. It was on those mornings that I got to know Marty, who soon discovered we shared another common interest. He heard that I worked with disadvantaged youth and was delighted to find out that, like him, I tried to incorporate the outdoors with them whenever possible. His eyes lit up and we shared an immediate bond that only folks who have seen a teenager respond to nature for the first time can appreciate.

I took advantage of the opportunity to pick his brain about the big mountains. This wasn't to be his first attempt on K2. Several years ago he had made it to high camp only before having to retreat, as is often the case on *"the Savage Mountain"*. He discussed the different 8000 meter giants in light of degree of difficulty. I suppose he knew my ulterior motive. I wanted to know how Broad Peak compared. He said, *"Broad Peak is a highly underrated mountain in terms of difficulty."* This made me feel better. I was now up to my neck in fixed rope, vertical climbing but it was also my first 8000er. From what I had read, other peaks at least seemed to relent on occasion. Marty confirmed this for me and made a final comment that I will remember forever. *"Broad Peak is a good one but K2 is the 'mountaineer's mountain."* With that he turned his head in direction of the peak, now totally obscured by clouds through an opening in the dining tent. He didn't have to say much more about this beautiful giant. He was going to press full on as soon as they finished Broad Peak. The gleam in his eye was undeniable.

Within a few days both Father and son reached the true summit of Broad Peak, two of 8 humans to successfully do so this year in a season that found experienced Sherpa turning back. It was to be the last summit the Schmidt duo would ever enjoy.

FLIGHT OF THE VALKYRIES

July 12, 2013

Figure 38: Scott Powrie heralds the arrival of rescue helicopters.
Photo John Quillen

Scott was integral to the evacuation, especially considering it was his satellite phone. I daresay that several hundred dollars' worth of calls went back and forth in what was to become a weeklong ordeal. His wife was equally vital keeping our friends and families involved. Unbeknownst to me, Joanna was providing all the folks in East Tennessee with constant updates and had befriended Raheel Adnan with Altitude Pakistan who kept a running blog about all the expeditions to the region. His information was the most comprehensive on the subject as I was to learn in later, more tragic days.

Zoltan, base camp manager, saunters lazily over to us at 9 a.m. on day six to deliver the good news. Our choppers are on their way. It is a perfect day cemented because I did not roll up my sleeping bag and pad. I fall down the now malformed platform that has melted below my tent creating a shelf from which the lower portion of my legs dangled for several nights. My fear of not jinxing the operation has come to fruition. I scramble to assemble the remainder of my gear as two of our cook staff, Akbar and Kareem plus Scott and Aziz, our HAP grab the patient and tote Brian up to the newly improved landing pad instead of the one we had so laboriously flattened, moving individual rocks to bare dirt. We spend the better part of three hours on that, now abandoned project one week ago. Someone decided that our choice of helipad was somewhat close to adjacent boulders.

Figure 39: Brian is tended by kitchen staff as helicopters circle for landing. (Broad Peak emerges from a weeklong cloud veil in the background).
Photo John Quillen

I organize Brian's stuff, which remained in a state of perpetual evacuation, and we shift to a place some two hundred yards from base camp. The new landing pad is in the shadow of the newly created memorial to Dana, the German lady, who died as a result of the bamboo bridge. The Karakoram is full of similar memorials. As we prepare to depart, Brian leans over to me and says, "John, I want you to stay and finish this mountain." Behind him, as if on cue, the clouds part over the summit of Broad Peak and display a clear path to camp 3. Broad Peak is lifting her veil to tease me. In fact, we can see tiny dots that indicate climbers, ascending for their respective summit bids from camp 1 for a final night of rest before their longest day. Brian reminds me after our return what I said to him in reply. "No, Brian, I don't think that this mountain is done claiming victims."

I cannot explain my rationale for saying this except it was a gut feeling and not for myself personally. This mountain was trying to tell us something and I was listening. As we hustle out of the mess tent prison, the Iranians bid us farewell. They are visibly relieved that help has finally arrived. With that they will embark for camp 3 and their ultimate destiny. I honestly feel as if they want to make sure that Brian is on his way. My last interaction with the "young bucks" is a hug as each reaches out to say goodbye. I remember grabbing Aidin by the shoulders and saying, "Please be careful." He flashes that huge smile and shrugs dismissively, "It's all right, no worry, you go." Mojtaba gives us another high five and departs base camp for the final time. It is so eerie when I think of that day in retrospect and in light of subsequent events.

As the helicopters round Concordia the relief is palpable. Almost one week of anxiety is coming to an end. In testament to their integrity, Scott and Ron agree to have our gear and "Old Yeller" brought down from camp 2. I still harbor great doubt about whether the Pakistani military will let me accompany Brian. Both machines pass overhead and buzz K2 basecamp to determine the prevailing wind. It seems to take about ten minutes. When the helicopter finally appears it banks in slowly and sets down in some wind. I jump in, holding Brian's head in my lap along with two backpacks. The two military pilots barely notice us and began powering up the machine to a violent rumble. We wave goodbye to our team and base camp attendants who crouch down amidst the boulders and glacial scree. Our uniformed pilot releases what looks like an emergency brake and we gain some ten feet of altitude. The machine teeters from side to side as the engine noise increases before slamming violently back to the ground. Very gently the pilot looks back around and tells me that we are too heavy and I have to get out. (At over 15,000 feet, we are testing the limits of these machines lift potential in the super thin air.) With that both me and my backpack are ejected from the aircraft. I crouch as my partner departs towards Concordia and eventually home. My fate is much less certain. I will admit that for a full minute I squat there staring at my team members who look at me in disbelief. I really can't believe what this potentially means. I feel like Wily Coyote after he lights a short fuse on some acme dynamite.

Knowing that there is another helicopter nearby, I frantically wave to them as they round the corner from K2 basecamp. Much to my relief, it lands to retrieve me. This machine has little trouble lifting in the 15000 foot air and soon we are buzzing our compound, home for the past month. Rounding Concordia, the full range of the Karakoram comes into view on a ride about which most humans can only dream. I shoot video of the entire event having realized days ago that my still camera has been somehow swallowed by Broad Peak during the ordeal with Brian. (All pictures credited to me in this book are a result of stills snatched from a go pro video camera) We are less than one hundred feet above the trail upon which we had sweated so heavily 30 days prior. I can see the Lilliputian porters, mules and trekkers ascending into the area. Like ants they march up to replenish expeditions from K2 to the Gasherbrum. It is amazing the landscape across which we had threaded our way to the upper reaches of this glacier. It resembles Mars or some other planet from above. The inhospitable geography becomes a maze of razor blades and I am very thankful not to be retreating down it on foot. Still, the beauty of these mountains is undeniable and I relish every second of this $16,000 air taxi.

Figure 40: We fly over our basecamp and my tent that had been home for so long.
Photo John Quillen

We soon circle what I recognized as Paiyu, or Pee yu as Brian and I came to know it. I remember it as the place where all the animal slaughtering took place and we made a dispatch for FTA on the heels of the Nanga Parbat tragedy.

Figure 41: Retracing our steps through the Throne Room.
Photo John Quillen

Circling the military outpost, we soon land in the lower elevation and I am offloaded to considerable heat from the midday sun. I am still wearing glacier clothing. It had been undeniably cold in base camp with all the bad weather the preceding week. I rarely removed my down parka and slept in it most nights wishing that "Old Yeller" were not so high on the mountain. The pilots escort me to a small building where there are chairs and a table. They motion for me to sit down and an uncharacteristically potbellied Pakistani moves up behind me. In my mind, he is the enforcer and I prepare to have what is left of my fingernails removed. There is this awkward pause as four uniformed Pakistani military officers circle a table and take respective seats. Staring me down without a word one of them eventually leans over and utters, "Will you join us in some tea?"

Meanwhile, Brian's whereabouts are unknown. I imagine they are wrenching his leg sideways to extort information while they play good cop with me. After 45 minutes of pleasantries, the officers ask if I would like to see Brian and escort me over to a bunkhouse where he is lying on a bed entertaining the cook staff with tales, likely at my expense. (This bunkhouse could have been straight off a 50's Western movie set. It is an adobe like hut with no windows and two rusted beds with springs and a mattress that looks like it has been in a 19th century brothel.) These pilots have all trained in the US at varying places such as Florida and Texas. They speak perfect English and exhibit typical Pakistani hospitality. One of the guys conveys some definite opinions about America and our war with the Taliban which gives me pause about whether or not I want to continue on his machine. After another round of tea and some fried chicken wings, the four pilots depart. One of the officers says, "We will be back in an hour and a half. Make yourself comfortable."

They return to Concordia minus us for the purpose of retrieving the body of Dana, the German climber who fell from the bridge. We have more tea and chicken wings until they return, at which point the antique stove is again lit for another round of tea. Subsequent to that, we once again board for departure to Skardu. This time Brian and I are placed on the same helicopter (with the opinionated pilot); the elevation is more conducive to lift off here at 9,000 feet or so. We follow the first helicopter with the body of the German and continue towards Askole. Thirty minutes after departure we lose sight of the first helicopter. Circling back towards the Baltoro we soon spot our escort parked on the ground two hundred feet below. They are forced to land in the middle of the trail for maintenance reasons. We circle back to set down as well in the middle of the high desert until they can change the fuel filter on their machine. Apparently the barrels of gasoline out there in the desert are prone to sand infiltration. And to think we were worried about Taliban.

Figure 42: Author visits crew of disabled helicopter.
Photo Brian Moran

Our chariots power back up after 40 minutes, maintenance issue resolved and continue down the Indus River to Skardu, passing Askole and the compound from which we had departed so many weeks ago; such short work of a trek that previously had involved so much effort. Soon we are following the serpentine jeep road upon which we bounced for ten hours on approach. I can see other vehicles negotiating the rocky gorges and rickety, one lane bridges. Approaching Skardu the green, lushness of the valley is apparent as we ring the military hospital. We barely touch down before Brian and I are discharged from the bird and rushing into the complex. I wave goodbye to our escorts as they bank the helicopter back toward base. I run behind the stretcher bearing my partner to the emergency room as the rotor wash pushes the hood of my jacket up over my head.

X-RAYS, GOATS AND FIRST CLASS SEATING

Skardu military hospital is the highest level of care available in the area. It is a compound of several buildings amongst which, different goat herds freely roam. Inside the "ER" is a room reminiscent of the Amityville Horror house with that many flies on the windows. The physician has to shoo them just to put Brian's x-ray up to read. (No, they didn't have one of those machines) It is evident that we are going to get Brian casted here and nothing else. I promised him that from the outset. It is clear to see multiple fractures and trauma to his ankle. He is soon wheeled on a gurney across the goat riddled compound where technicians place him in a cast from his foot to the hip. We encourage hospital staff to keep him overnight (bribe is too strong of a word.) This will fulfill the requirements from Global Rescue which stipulate an overnight stay in a hospital. (The thought of having to ingest the evacuation bill over this technicality was much anticipated. Naik Nam from ATP was there every step of the way from touch down till departure. I believe that Brian's total hotel bill was less than one hundred dollars.) After a few hours we say goodbye to Brian and ATP takes me 35 minutes across town to the familiar Concordia motel. It feels like home away from home. The owner raises his big, grey eyebrows at my return and I have a long story to tell before I can slip away for the shower about which I have been constantly fantasizing.

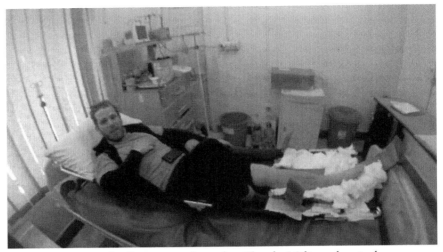

Figure 43: Brian is evaluated at Skardu Military hospital.
Photo John Quillen

Relishing in what can only be described as the best bathing experience of my life (It lasts 30 minutes and the hot water is plentiful). I call the States much to the relief of my Mother who answers the phone. She is very relieved and conveys our safe arrival to the family. I got hold of my Dad who was also awaiting news of our escape from the Karakoram but reminds me that we are still "in enemy territory." That brings back thoughts of the Nanga Parbat incident which have been forcibly pushed to the back of our collective conscience. I rush to call Joanna and it is reassuring to hear her voice as well. Soon I am in a hurry to catch dinner at the hotel. Before me soon are fresh food and vegetables and a comfortable real seat overlooking the Indus River. I sip a sugary coke while gazing across the sandy shoals of beach upon which I had carved a track in my afternoon runs so many weeks before. So much had transpired in the weeks since I last dined here anticipating an effortless run to the summit of K3. The water from those shoals originated atop the peaks we had roamed for so long. It is as if our blood is intertwined with that river. Guests regard me like a walking corpse with my weathered and gaunt face as I hide in a corner of the dining room with my thoughts.

I collapse like a corpse that evening and early the next morning ATP returns to gather me so we can collect Brian. This trip lasts until lunchtime. For some arbitrary reason my entrance into the facility this day is prohibited. Goats are okay but not Americans. It is apparent that a few rupees can open the swinging bar but out of principle I decline opting instead to wait for two hours in the heat with the free ranging goats during Ramadan. I learn an important lesson here regarding Muslim culture. As I stand on the dusty street enjoying another warm bottle of coca cola, I am yelled at by several young men. Apparently, it is disrespectful to eat or drink from sunup to sundown during this period.

When they wheel Brian out in an ambulance, I board and off we go. Negotiating the crowded Skardu streets we encounter what appears to be a large demonstration of young, angry men. They are marching towards our ambulance chanting in unison. One of them begins banging on our vehicle. I immediately presume there has been some fresh drone strike and these Pakistanis are looking for Americans. Naik Nam assures me that they are just school boys who are upset with some change in curriculum. I make sure that Brian's head is below their field of vision.

Thirty five minutes later we are back at the Concordia and Brian is offloaded to great excitement from hotel staff. With the assistance of ATP and hotel staff, we wheel him into the room. He is anxious to find a way to shower and suggests that we order some French fries, having figured out long ago it is hard to mess them up. Hotel staff produces a pair of rickety crutches that look like they could have been used in the civil war. They require reinforcing as the supports have deteriorated and are missing rubber tips. As I shoulder Brian onto the floor of the bathroom, one of those sticks blows out on the slick tile and we nearly have another tragedy with which to contend. Brian is able to simultaneously grab my shoulder and a plastic chair I have placed for him to sit while bathing.

We relax sipping soft drinks and shooing flies from French fries until dinner, also brought to our room. Another surprise is that ATP collects us for a return visit to the hospital. They have apparently decided to remove his cast and put on a shorter one to facilitate air travel. I am getting tired of the hospital and consider letting him go alone. But I go anyway; it isn't like I have a heavy schedule for the day. This time I am allowed to enter the goat riddled facility where I sit on the street between out buildings from which Brian eventually emerges after some yelling sporting a shorter cast. "Did you hear me screaming in there?"

"No," I replied, "Was it that bad?"
"Yes, it was ten times worse than the first time!"

He did have a more mobile version of the full cast. Hospital staff pour from the building to inspect the artisan's handiwork on Brian's leg. From the white, sticky hands of a moustached professional comes a smile of contentment with his efforts. I presume that Naik Nam has orchestrated this for Brian's convenience. We then return to the hotel for what I hope is a final trip through the dusty Skardu streets. That evening I wheel him to the dining room where we enjoy a nice dinner of curried chicken and watermelon for desert. The internet is functioning now and Brian makes calls to his family who are obviously quite relieved. As I push him back into the hotel room my pants fall to the floor. I have lost 18 pounds since the start of this expedition and it definitely shows. My shoulder bones are protruding and gone is my little belly pouch.

The next morning brings a wonderful surprise. After wheeling my partner to the dining room for an early coffee, Brian reads an email from Global Rescue which indicates that they are going to fly both of us home, first class, the following day. I have to re-read it three times myself to believe this wonderful news. All the bad luck seems to be nearing an end. Yawer's assertions prove accurate as ATP secures a flight to Islamabad from Skardu despite our fears that we may have to yet again endure the 30-hour bus ride along the Karakoram Highway. It is smooth, but long sailing from Skardu to Islamabad. Ironically, seated next to Brian on the small airplane is the guy who has put both casts on his leg. In order to get Brian onto the plane, we have to pick him up and carry him from the tarmac and up the steps of the aircraft. This is Pakistan's version of handicapped accessibility which was to be repeated again later in Islamabad. We pass over the snowy flanks of Nanga Parbat. In Urdu the pilot heralds the majesty of this deadly giant through the loudspeaker. Pakistanis regard this peak almost religiously. It is their crown jewel of a mountain. For me it is yet another reminder of the perils from which I was spared by the grace and majesty of God in a place that sometimes seems forsaken.

Figure 44: Nanga Parbat from airplane.
Photo Brian Moran

After a one and a half hour flight I find myself again in the hot, stale baggage claim with the motionless fans high in airless windows. The power has stopped, just as I left it weeks earlier. Nothing has changed, like many things in this country. I oversee the men who carry Brian into this terminal and collect our things which, thankfully, do all arrive this time,

Figure 45: Ashraf Aman assists Brian at Benazir Bhutto airport in Rawalpindi.
Photo John Quillen

Ashraf Aman is patiently waiting to shepherd us back to the Envoy Continental hotel. Ashraf is quite gracious and by now great friends with Brian following their time obtaining the visa extension at the beginning of the trip. He has arranged a room for us to accommodate a 6-hour layover. With Brian's arms on my shoulder and the useless crutches we were given in Skardu, Brian limps upstairs to the tiny closet that passes for lodging in Islamabad's Blue Zone. Neither of us are complaining. We shower and prepare for three long flights back to the states. We also order some more French fries. Soon we are saying goodbye to Ashraf for the final time and boarding a 747 that pilot Brian informs me is over thirty years old. We settle into the nose section at the top. Boarding a five and a half hour flight to Jeddah, Saudi Arabia, it is soon apparent that we are the only people aboard who are not wearing robes and sandals in commemoration of Ramadan. The flight attendant takes our food order but reminds us that the rest of the passengers will not be dining until after sunset in commemoration of this holy period. The flight attendant offers to serve our meal but we defer to our hosts and dine only after the sun takes its final bow over a shrinking Arabian skyline.

There are layovers in Jeddah and another leg to Paris. First class has its advantages for sure. We make sure that Brian has a comfortable leg position but he is still obviously in some pain and running low on morphine pills. In Paris two very nice women help wheel him from the gate to the lounge where we enjoy a full French breakfast buffet. The Western world into which we are now immersed with pristine, modern airports and food aplenty seems strange and foreign to me. I still expect to see an errant goat crossing my periphery.

There is little difficulty for me resting most of the way back. When we reach Atlanta there is a small, unfortunate incident. Customs forces us to enter a glass room when they discover that we have been to Pakistan and Brian is an airline pilot who purchased a last minute ticket to the most dangerous country on earth. Immigration officials direct us to this room as I wheel Brian into a waiting area filled with international arrivals. There are no other US citizens in this area. I stand there for about five minutes realizing that no one is paying attention to us outside so I head back for the sliding glass door. As I approach the electric, sliding wall of glass, nothing happens. That door is one way and locked. I am infuriated and begin banging on the door. To have been through all that we have endured and be locked up on our return to the States is the final straw. I go off on some immigration officer and have few regrets about doing so. I remind him that my perception of US law prohibits incarceration of American citizens. I continue banging on the glass and make sure every traveler passing freely is aware of what they are doing to us. They finally open the door and some guy suggests that I go and retrieve our luggage. I do just that and return to collect Brian. They have apparently worked things out in my absence but it doesn't change the fact that we were locked up with no probable cause in our home country.

Still steaming, I roll Brian in a wheelchair into the baggage claim since no airline employees in Atlanta seemed interested in doing so. (Unlike in Jeddah and Paris where polite and concerned staff shepherded my friend from place to place, the ground staff in Atlanta just point to a wheelchair as we disembark.) There is Brian's family waiting patiently and very relieved to see us both. They have signs welcoming both of us back home. We joyously embrace the group. Present with Brian's patient wife, Ashley are Brian's mother, Becky, sister Jennifer, nephew Peter and stepfather Larry. It is a warm occasion. Ashley has arranged a doctor's appointment that afternoon with Brian's orthopedic surgeon. I feel sorry for Ashley knowing she will be having to care for an immobile dude that is ordinarily hyperactive in the first place.

Brian is able to hook me up with one of his buddy pass seats to Knoxville. I am going to be home within two hours. I leave my climbing buddy to begin his journey of treatment and healing from Broad Peak. Obviously, he has a long row to hoe. By midafternoon I land in Knoxville and Joanna is there to collect me, somewhat lighter and more harry than when I departed on June 10. She is a sight for sore eyes. I'm unsure of exactly how long we have been traveling but I believe that our in airtime from Islamabad was 27 hours. This doesn't count the helicopter and airplane out of Skardu.

DASHING THROUGH DANGER

I struggled with the transition back to civilization. It seemed as if one minute I was flipping snow crusted boulders with my ice axe looking for suitable toilets or meltable ice and the next sitting in my easy chair surfing the web for information. Trading pre-dawn wake ups for leisurely, gourmet coffee mornings, I followed the events of our remaining expedition members with great anticipation. The day following our departure, Ron and Scott set off for their summit bid and within two days arrived at camp 3. They joined Ramin and Afshin who followed Aidin, Mojtaba and Pouya who were one day ahead of everyone else's schedule. Scott and Ron set up about 50 meters below Ramin and Afshin. Aidin, Mojtaba and Pouya split from the group to begin in earnest completion of the "Iranian" route to the summit. From camp 3 they traversed to the right and planned to make a couple of bivouac campsites before tagging the top and descending via the normal route. We all expected that this would take a few days.

In the meantime Scott and Ron continued their journey on the standard route as Ramin and Afshin monitored the summit assault of their countrymen from camp 3. Unfortunately, Scott fell into a small crevasse shortly outside of camp 3 and made a decision to retreat. Ron continued for the summit but did not reach the true summit, only the false summit a couple of hours below. Not that it is any small achievement. The false summit rises to 8000 meters and is a monumental feat on a mountain that had only seen about two total summits to date this season. Ron later informed me that his round trip from camp 3 to the false summit was 20 hours. "I took a little nap near a rock outcropping, which is probably something you shouldn't do." Ron later confessed. Considering his usual pace that time is remarkable. Given that he was typically at least thirty percent faster than me I could have expected an epic summit attempt. I kept close tabs on Mojtaba, Aidin and Pouya. They were making a bold run on dangerous, virgin ground; the inherent risks of their plan were well understood and I'm confident there was no absence of anxiety among their support team.

Figure 46: left to right: Pouya, Aidin and Mojtaba at lower camp 1.
Photo Iranian Team Archives

On July 15th, after a bivouac at 24,114 feet, the Three Musketeers forged onward as they transitioned off the snowfields onto vertical rock. It was also during this time that they managed to connect with Ramin and Afshin at camp 3. These are Ramin's words regarding his conversation with them at that point:

> *I reached camp 3 at 9 a.m. and managed to talk to them at 9:20. Aidin was on the radio and I strongly recommended they should leave their loads behind, go for the summit as fast as they could, and descend from the same route they'd climbed. Aidin rejected this idea as he thought they had to rappel all the way down, which to his mind was difficult and time consuming.*

At 11 a.m. I tried to convince them again and told them: "it's not a 4000m traverse. The weather may get even worse and you're going to descend from normal route which is unknown to you while you are familiar with your own route." they rejected my idea again.

Figure 47: Mojtaba descends from upper part of K3.
Photo Iranian Team archives

That must have been an incredible day for them because they only made about 900 feet of elevation but were now less than 16 feet shy of the magic 8000 meter mark (26,246 feet). I suspect that all of their technical rock and ice skills came into play as they etched their way to just 154 feet shy of the summit. It is during these times that your altimeter can become an enemy, pushing you to reach a number in defiance of the objective hazards. The last section before the summit is purported to be 75 degree ice.

Figure 48: site of Iranian camps on new route to summit.
Photo Ramin Shojaei

Ramin conveyed,

> *At around 1 p.m. they told me they were just 1 hour below the summit.*
> *It turned out they had estimated wrongly. At 7:30 p.m. we talked again.*
> *They still believed they were just 45 minutes below the summit. They*
> *had estimated they would reach the summit in half an hour, and it took*
> *5-6 hours in reality. The sky was clear that night*

On July 16th it appears as if the Three Musketeers overcame all obstacles and planted the Iranian flag that had marked our compound on the summit of Broad Peak. I could mentally picture the celebration those boys had on the summit of this, the earth's 12th highest peak that afternoon with the realization of their accomplishment and recognition of Iran and the world climbing community.

The following day, things went horribly wrong. Subsequent triangulation of satellite phone calls placed their position off the normal route. Aidin was calling for a rescue but no one knew where they were. And the weather was getting bad again. We later discovered that they had dropped off the front of the mountain, unable to intersect the normal route. The lack of traffic and constant snowfall obscured the "standard" path they hoped to follow to safety. Dropping down they apparently realized their mistake after hitting an insurmountable wall. Out of fuel and food and having lost their tent in the wind, our friends were in big trouble. Big trouble at 8000 meters is like no other kind of trouble. Helicopters cannot go that high in Pakistan or anywhere else for that matter despite what one company asserts was a landing on Mt. Everest. (It is generally considered a hoax).

Figure 49: Satellite phone triangulation of Iranian's last location on K3.
Photo Ramin Shojaei

On July 18th a couple of the Polish climbers were evacuated from the mountain for severe frostbite. This would seem to vindicate Shojaei's decision to turn back and avoid the same fate. It was also on this day that Aidin made another, desperate satellite phone call. He told folks in Iran that one of team mates had already passed and another was in dire straits. According to Ramin Shojaei, Aidin said, "If nobody helps me I will become like the other two." They were out of fuel and food. During that time porters moved towards the summit to look for signs of the Iranians. However, they were so far off route it wasn't a practical expectation. Ramin was on the ground organizing efforts to rescue his countrymen. Shojaei related," I felt absolutely heartbroken. I envisioned myself as a mother whose kid is under a heavy rock and she can't lift it. And the only thing she can do is to watch her kid suffer." He succeeded in getting a military helicopter to buzz the area at the limits of its operating capacity with a seasoned high altitude climber, Thomas Laemmle, aboard. Laemmle is a high altitude physiologist in addition to being a climbing guide. He was suited up with oxygen prepared to execute a rescue, if possible. Unfortunately they found no signs of the Iranians. ATP called off rescue efforts the following day. Many anxious days passed with no word. Ramin, Afshin Azim and Ron remained in our base camp fueling hope and rotating up the mountain to higher camps. At one point, Marty and Denali Schmidt headed towards the heights to assist but turned around after being told by someone in the medical field that there was little likelihood of survival at this point.

BULLDOG ON THE GROUND

Figure 50: Ramin Shojaei directs rescuer Thomas Laemmle using maps of their route (Ron Hoglin is in the background looking on and Ganga is in the blue jacket.)

Photo permission Thomas Laemmle

Online efforts to petition the Pakistanis to resume rescue efforts paid off and on July 21 another helicopter search was initiated. This was after the newly elected President of Iran intervened. Laemmle's detailed pictures of the area had triangulated what they felt was the position of Aidin's last satellite phone call. It was apparent that the Iranians had descended the wrong route from the summit and hit a huge, impassable wall. There was no sign of them anywhere. High altitude porters who made it to the summit found the Iranian flag planted atop the mountain but no sign of the owners. They did find a body but believed it to belong to one of the Poles who perished on Broad Peak the previous winter. K3, it appeared, was threatening three more lives in a year that had already seen that many claimed.

Our team leader, Ron Hoglin, stayed in base camp with Ramin, Afshin and Azim to assist in the rescue efforts. Scott departed for Askole immediately after returning to base camp, having no idea of the Iranian's plight. I can only imagine the stress, anxiety and sadness that filled our mess tent during those days following our departure. As Brian and I spoke back and forth between Georgia and Tennessee we thought of Ramin. If ever you were to have someone in that position to keep hope alive, we agreed that Ramin was the man. He was level headed, stern and would not take no for an answer.

Particularly illustrative of that point is what happened one day on our 100 mile plus trek to K3 base camp. Team members noted that our prepared lunches were somewhat lacking. Given the amount of caloric output in addition to the strenuous level of hiking, small rations of cheese, nuts and a boiled egg burned off quickly on our 10-hour days. Ramin approached Sher Ali to request more food. Apparently Sher Ali's response was insufficient. What we heard coming from the cook tent was Ramin's emphatic statement to the cook staff, "That is not good enough. We need more food." The following day our rations were nearly doubled. I started calling him "The Enforcer" and he immediately gained my unwavering respect. In fact, when we were debating the merits of putting Brian on porters versus waiting for the helicopter, I enlisted the advice of Ramin who agreed that Brian should not be moved down the glacier. "I think it is better if you stay here and wait," Ramin pensively suggested. Brian respected his opinion equally and with that we remained in base camp and informed Global Rescue to remove this option from the table.

This is Ramin's account of the days preceding Aidin, Pouya and Mojtaba's disappearance:

I estimated that the route would take 2 days to finish. One day to the end of technical difficulties at around 7350m, and one day to the summit. We decided that summit team should carry another day of fuel and food just in case. Descent would be from normal route, or if it made sense, the same route they had climbed. Aidin and others had told me that in 2011 fixing rope to the end of traverse had taken around 5 hours.

This time they didn't require fixing so I thought it would take even less time. Also, they would use ATC Guide belay device so that two would be belayed at the same time. They shared a 2 person tent, with no fly, among themselves. Aidin and Mojtaba preferred to have down jacket and sleeping bag and Pouya just down jacket and pant.

July 13th was the first day to tackle new route. Summit team started their climb at 7 a.m. By 5 p.m. they had reached only to the end of traverse. Aidin told me on the radio that ice condition was worse than two years ago. They had specially faced difficult terrain on a rock-ice section. It was obvious they would not reach 7350m that day. There was a small col at around 7050m that they could pitch their tent. They reached there at around 7:30 p.m. and stayed for the night.

I and Afshin climbed from camp 2 to camp 3 that same day. We hoped to climb normal route next day and possibly greet the other 3 on the summit. But now we decided to wait at camp 3 and start our own climb the next day.

The morning of July 14th I talked to other three and Aidin told me they didn't rest well last night as the ledge was small and they could only sit. I warned them to be careful not to lose their concentration due to lack of sleep. But they started strong with good spirit. It was rather steep ice and it took them another day before they reached 7250m to a place where they could build a platform for their tent and rest well for the night.

First thing I asked was about snow/ice condition; it was snow and not ice anymore.

I and Afshin prepared ourselves for our summit bid that afternoon. It was a cold and very windy night. I woke up at 12 midnight. Two Polish climbers passed beside our tent and I followed an hour later. Afshin didn't have adequate clothing and felt very cold after a few meters. So he decided to stay. I was fast and didn't feel cold at all.

The weather, however, was not cooperating with Shojaei and before long he was forced to retreat back to camp 3. His fingers and toes were feeling the cold. According to Ramin he was more concerned about the three team members and tried to stay in radio contact with Mojtaba. By nine am, Ramin was back in camp and by 9:20 had contacted Aidin. *(This was the conversation where Shojaei tried to convince them to retrace their ascent route since it was familiar.)*

Back home in Knoxville I was compulsively glued to the computer scanning reports from the field and on Raheel Adnan's Altitude Pakistan blog. Field Touring had stopped posting dispatches of any significance following the Nanga Parbat murders, according to FTA representative Stu Remensnyder, to avoid broadcasting our movements. In my heart I knew that if there were any hope, that Aidin would have frostbite and likely lose most fingers and toes. But the reality was starting to sink in. Chances of their survival were minimal at this point. I couldn't wrap my mind around the concept that these three guys may never be coming back from Broad Peak. I got angry with the mountain. She had claimed enough lives and limbs this year.

Ramin continues:

At around 10 a.m., they had contacted Ron at base camp and told him they could not find fixed rope on the normal route and were asking for direction. Ron, who had climbed to the rocky summit a few days earlier tried to guide them the best he could. Ron remembers they were talking about a yellow band which was surprising to him. He could not remember such a thing.

It wasn't until subsequent conversations with Ramin and Ron that I got some of the back-story on Aidin's last phone call. It was information that clouded my imagery of the boys on the peak. Ramin conveyed that when Aidin called on the 18th he thought he was near camp four and saw a tent. *(I never found out if any teams actually made a camp four this year and Ron seemed to imply that he had passed no tents on his summit bid).* He also described seeing a blue fixed rope that he could not reach. That is when the two HAPs struck for the summit in hopes of locating him. *(Those two porters were loaned to the rescue effort by our team member Ganga. It was an act of selflessness that ensured she would have to abandon her own attempt. Sarvar and Asghat reached the true summit but found no signs of Aidin, Pouya or Mojtaba. They did find the Iranian flag and a body presumed to be one of the Poles. They were strong and acclimatized.)* In all, Ramin made three attempts to strike for the summit from camp 3 in hopes of intercepting the three and Afshin returned for another attempt during which he fell into the glacial river from the bamboo bridge of death nearly getting hypothermia in the process.

I asked Ron if he knew whether or not Mojtaba and Pouya were still alive at this point. It had been bothering me to think about Aidin sitting there with Mojtaba or Pouya already dead. Ron paused before telling me that Aidin said they had both already passed. He was wandering the mountain alone and likely hallucinating. Only God knows what those three truly endured during their ten days at the top of the world.

KING CHOGORI EXACTS HIS TOLL.

K2 Camp 3 July 26, 203

Figure 51: Marty and Denali Schmidt

After trying unsuccessfully to assist in the rescue of the Iranians, Marty Schmidt, son Denali and team mate Chris Warner departed for nearby K2. They waited out the storm periods that had sealed the Iranian's fate on Broad Peak. Having been successfully acclimatized from the Broad Peak ascent, all three decided to push up during a storm and place themselves in alignment for a summit bid with the next clearing weather pattern at camp 2 on K2.

Team mate Chris Warner related the following account of events:

> *I write to you so you may have a better understanding of what happened here in Pakistan with Marty and Denali rather than hearing stories through the media and the hearsay of others. Most of you would have known them better than I did. I first met Marty in 2004 on Cho Oyu*

135

and Denali I met on this trip. Expeditions are intense little periods of living together and we learn a lot about others as well as ourselves. In my 18 years of climbing this is the most tragic of accidents I have personally experienced.

We were a small team of three with the idea of climbing Broad Peak and then an alpine style ascent of K2, this was my second attempt on K2. Broad Peak was the mountain we would acclimatize on and get us prepared as a team for K2. We had a very comfortable and straight forward ascent of this mountain and summited it within 3 weeks of arriving. Both Marty and Denali were climbing strong on the mountain with Denali showing all the talent of his father, he had his father's legs, lungs and heart. It was inspiring to watch an 8000m novice climb with such ease.

They were both very much liked in base camp and their characters both showed true with the two following incidences.

A few days before our summit bid on Broad Peak a German woman died on another team and both Marty and Denali volunteered to climb to camp 2 and retrieve equipment for the other members as they were now canceling their expedition. They both carried about 30kg down each of other people's gear. A massive effort for the benefit of others just a few days before our summit bid.

Then later after our summit we moved up the glacier 1 hours walk to K2 base camp. Just on arriving there we heard that an Iranian expedition had three members missing near the summit, we had camped with them at camp 3 and watched them climb up their new route. So on the motivation of Marty we packed our rucksacks and headed back down to Broad Peak and started climbing up the mountain again to look for them at the col. The rescue attempt sadly was soon called off as we had misinformation about where the three were and the possibility of finding them now without danger to our lives was too great. They were somewhere around 7600m on a new route and had been lost for about four days already. So we descended the mountain once again and returned to K2 base camp.

Now we concentrated on our push for the summit of K2 and had a good weather window coming with an idea to summit on the 28 of July. Most all the other teams in base camp were also going for this summit window. We could then all share the work of getting to camp four and then again to the summit with carrying rope and breaking trail in the snow.

We left for camp 2 direct on the 25th July reaching there just after midday. We were carrying 260m of rope for fixing the bottle neck and were packed for a single push to the summit, just four days food and one tent that we would move up as we climbed. We all felt strong, healthy and acclimatized.

That evening as we sat cooking and resting in our tent we heard word that the Sherpa's from other teams had failed to make camp 3 by only a few 100 meters. This was due to the snow conditions and took a long nine hour day from camp 2. They were carrying a deposit of equipment for their teams (mostly oxygen) and then returning to camp 2 that same day to then continue back up on our same schedule. It had been snowing lightly all afternoon and we got different reports of snow being 6ft deep, chest deep and waist deep. The Sherpas had tried to push through the snow but after small sloughs coming down on them and one Sherpa sliding down 10m they decided that it was too dangerous. All this snow sitting on a 30 degree slope of curving blue ice.

Before we knew it many teams started descending past our tent canceling their summit bid and expedition all together. We had only just got on the mountain and everyone was bailing with very little discussion. Our shared manpower and rope was quickly going down the mountain, all three of us surprised.

Marty was encouraging people to stay and wait at camp 2. To let the snow settle. Some agreed but they descended anyway. That night we decided that we all would go up and just see how conditions really were. It was good fitness and acclimatization and we can make a deposit and try again in a few weeks if need be.

By morning I had changed my mind. It had snowed lightly most of the night, and everyone else was descending so I didn't believe that the three of us could make trail to the summit in such snow. I felt it was better to simply descend and rest, then wait for the next weather window rather than push into new snow. Marty and Denali didn't flinch, they said ok to my decision and were adamant about continuing up. We sorted the gear again as they were going lighter in loads, reducing the food to two days but taking some extra screws, stakes and only 60m of 7mm rope. Both Marty and Denali were in the same frame of mind. One did not convince the other to go up, they were both motivated and prepared to assess the conditions and turn around if need be. So at around 9 a.m. on the 26th I swallowed my ego and descended from camp 2 feeling that I had blown my summit chance as these two were heading to the top.

I arrived back at base camp that day and waited eagerly for their six p.m. radio call. By 6.45 they radioed in, they had taken nine hours to reach camp 3. Marty was brief, he said it had been a hard day, that it was very windy with spindrift and that they were cold. He congratulated Denali as he had broken trail to camp 3 pushing through waist deep snow to 7200m. I asked what their plans were for the next day and he replied that he was unsure and that he would let me know in the morning with the 8 a.m. radio call. From base camp we could see the wind blowing at camp 3 and the spindrift coming off the shoulder. My feeling was that they would descend the next day.

Base camp was now getting divided as they had made camp 3 and some climbers were trying to rally a group to head back up and summit on the 1 August but this met with mixed feelings.

In the morning of the 27th of July several climbers came into our camp to hear Marty's decision, but 8 a.m. came and went with nothing. Why hadn't he called? Marty is very good with radio calls and rarely late (except for last night). So we waited, and before long in was 12 noon the next radio call but still nothing. Had he run out of battery? Dropped the radio, his pack? We're they descending? Concern came over base camp but too early to think a problem…? 6 p.m. came and still nothing on the radio. We all knew they were strong, capable and not the type to make bad decisions, they are going to walk into base camp any moment…we all went to bed worried and I slept with my radio on hoping.

The next day about six Sherpas and some Pakistani high altitude porters were heading up to camp 1 and two to get equipment and bring it down. Getting to camp 2 was no worry in the current snow conditions and it had only been snowing higher up. Two Sherpa's Mingma and Norbu were heading up to a deposit halfway between camp 2 and three to retrieve an oxygen mask and a few other things. So I talked with their leader and convinced them to continue all the way to camp 3. They had been part of the group that had turned around several days before. There was now many climbers low on the mountain keeping a lookout for Marty and Denali. If they were moving they would be found.

The Sherpa's climbed very quickly and by about 6.30 p.m. Mingma had reached camp 3 that same day from base camp. He radioed into his leader Lakpa and said that there had been a very large avalanche with a scar about 400m wide. He found a BD axe and BD crampons that matched the type both Marty and Denali had been using. There was no sign of them or their tent. Mingma said he felt scared with the conditions and it was getting dark. He took a few pictures and started descending.

This confirmed our fears that there had been an avalanche at camp 3 a well-known camp for avalanche. I believe that they would have been in their tent asleep when it happened. The fact that they did not have their crampons on suggests this and makes sense why they didn't make the 8 a.m. radio call which I would have expected to be done from inside their tent.

When Mingma returned the next day I talked with him some more and saw the pictures confirming the axes and crampons as those of Marty and Denali. It looked more like they were buried in their tent than swept down the mountain. Their death was truly a shock to the camp. So liked and so well regarded.

A few days later I made a plaque and we had a gathering at the Gilky memorial just near K2 base camp. A touching afternoon as all the climbers came to pay respect.

For days I still felt that the two of them would walk into camp, it just seemed so unreal that they had gone. I packed their belongings and the next day I walked out with the Greek expedition who we all spent a lot of time with. It was only then that it really began to sink in that they had both gone. The emotions filling my body the reality taking hold, I stared a long time at that mountain. Marty and Denali resting high on the ridge.

It was wonderful to be able to share time with them both in the mountains. To experience and be part of such a beautiful relationship, father and son.

There were now six people with whom we had spent time on this expedition that were never returning from the journey. I also found out from Scott and Ron that my tent had blown off the mountain at camp 2. It had mysteriously been the only tent to do so despite the weighting of all the rocks and gear. My sleeping bag, Old Yeller was also now officially a casualty of the Karakoram. It was as if the mountain were bitch slapping me from half way across the world since I was one of the few who escaped unharmed. It was, considering the alternatives and tragic circumstances, a palatable loss. We did finally receive confirmation that Tunc Findic had escaped the butchery on Nanga Parbat since he was at a higher camp when the murderers stormed base camp.

My still camera, however, was another tragedy. It disappeared during Brian's rescue somewhere. I presume it dislodged from the carrying case on my backpack which was handed back and forth several times during the ordeal. Gone were my prized shots of K2 and all the Karakoram grandeur. Such was the fate of any final photographic record of the three boys that had become our brothers.

ANGELS AND GHOSTS

When Brian and I returned from extreme Western China in 20011, just on the other side of K2, I had six months of recovery time and $17,500 worth of hyperbaric oxygen chamber visits that restored the ends of my fingers from black to a nice pinkish tint. It was a super cold summit day that saw the majority of our expedition turn back outside of camp 3 on Muztagh Ata on the Tash route that July. The temperature was well below zero and Brian had the good sense to retreat while I forged on. The result was a great deal of agony for my 22 hours of climbing, most of which was solo. I was fortunate in that I recovered from six frostbitten appendages with only a small permanent loss of feeling in the end of a finger or two. There were two Belgians that preceded me by one day on that mountain that fared much worse. It was apparent they would require amputation of their blackened hands and feet. For K3 I had amassed about four sets of gloves for varying occasions and two pounds of chemical hand warmers. I presume they are laying somewhere near Old Yeller in a couloir on the side of Broad Peak facing K2.

Three months after returning to the States and receiving medical care in Georgia, Brian had to return to the hospital for an infection in the shattered leg that was now held together with everything but bailing wire. He had 17 screws and two metal plates. He was now headed to the oxygen chamber for a different reason but the principal was the same. It is somewhat ironic that treatment from our high altitude oxygen deprived adventures was forced oxygen therapy upon return. It seems a mountaineering yin and yang.

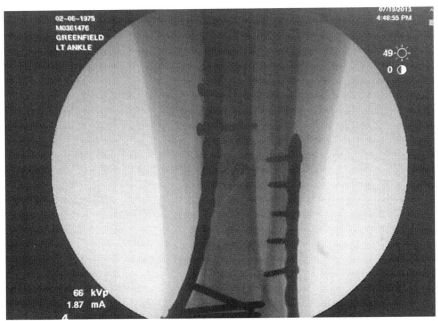

Figure 52: Brian's leg following the first of three procedures in which plates and screws secure his shattered leg.
Photo Brian Moran

On August 8, two Pakistani policemen pursuing leads in the Nanga Parbat massacre were gunned down while driving in the town of Chilas (the town about which we were warned and dutifully avoided upon our return. It was where we stayed in the hot hotel that resembled a dungeon.) Subsequently, on August 20 2013 Pakistani security officers raided a compound and arrested 20 suspects linked to the Nanga Parbat tragedy. The suspects generally considered the perpetrators of the massacre were also lounging about successfully in Chilas. It underscored the danger that I was personally able to avoid on a daily basis on this trip. News like this trickling in for weeks following our expedition started to give me pause about that dark figure at the bottom of the fixed ropes who led me to safety. No doubt I had a guardian angel and he was working overtime.

There are old climbers and there are bold climbers but there are no old bold climbers. That is a mountain saying that has never been truer than in the Karakoram in 2013. Of the 21 total deaths in the region that year, the largest number ever recorded in one climbing season in Pakistan, the majority were a result of bold moves. When Marty and Denali moved up in a snowstorm, it defied mountain logic. Then there were the Iranians who put up a very technical line on Broad Peak that will likely not be repeated any time soon.

Similarly, on Gasherbrum 1, Artur Hajzer fell while descending the Japanese couloir. Ironically, Hajzer, a Himalayan legend who abandoned the sport at age 28 because he could not endure the continuing loss of life amongst his climbing partners, had returned at age 51 to attempt both Gasherbrum 1 and 2. G1 saw a similar, unfortunate historical spike in mortality this particular year when you include the deaths of three Spaniards, Abel Alonso, Xevi Gomez and Alvaro Paredes. They became disoriented while descending from the summit and disappeared. One of their team did manage to stumble into camp and never saw his partners again.

I would not have joined the Iranians in their new route, however. Primarily because it was an Iranian project and second I was having sufficient difficulty with the "normal" route. Least important was the fact that I wasn't asked. Similarly, I had no intentions of moving on to K2, like Ganga and the Schmidt's should we have found success on Broad Peak. It would have been simple enough to coordinate but I was realistic about my first 8000 meter attempt. Many people have asked about these details and I need to point out that all the aforementioned deaths were the result of bold moves on dangerous ground. Many have also speculated that Brian's injury may have prevented worse happenings for us higher up on the mountain. God alone knows that answer. Eight people reached the summit of Broad Peak in 2013. Three were the Iranians and two were the Schmidt family.

When Jon Krakauer returned home from his 1996 Everest climb that was filled with tragedy and deaths of team mates he was counseled to wait a couple of years before penning his thoughts. As a result, he made some mistakes that were corrected over time. Like Krakauer, writing of these events has been an emotional catharsis for me. The events on Broad Peak and nearby were gnawing my guts out as well. He thought that by penning his account it would purge the mountain from his life. It was, of course, a fallacy to which we both likely have fallen victim.

How does one gain perspective on this tragedy and all the perfect storm of ugliness that hung over the Broad Peak and the Karakoram in general during our expedition? As time passes so will our perceptions and the reasons will become clearer as outlined in a general purpose for God's will on this expedition. One day while we were attempting one of the many failed satellite phone calls to the Global Rescue office, Mojtaba was prattling on quite animated in the background while Brian struggled to piece together broken phrases through the phone held so closely to his face. We both grimaced as Mojtaba intently conversed with Aidin and Pouya. From our vantage point it appeared as if they were arguing. Either way, Mojtaba had to make a point. As the conversation was in Farsi and gaining in volume Brian was losing his battle to make sense out of an evacuation plan through one of the few successful satellite connections. The Three Musketeers knew what was transpiring during Brian's phone conversation and they carried on quite uncharacteristically. As I watched Mojtaba gesturing with his hands and the reactions of his other teammates, the thought crossed both our heads to tell them to tone it down until Brian finished with Global Rescue. For some reason, neither of us could bring ourselves to do so. It seemed like Mojtaba had a lot to say in a short amount of time and we just winked at each other and ignored them. I think he would have had a lot of words to say in his unfulfilled years on this planet and I regret that none will ever hear them.

I can say that the most positive aspect of this climb for me includes the time I spent with the Iranians. It was a blessing to be with these boys during their final days and it will remain with me forever. Also I cannot say enough about the Balti people and their hospitality. Never once was I treated disrespectfully and most of the time it was with genuine warmth and first class hospitality. The Pakistanis take great pride in treating foreigners better than family. I refuse to let the actions of some redneck Taliban color my perception of the entire culture. As our cook, Sher Ali said, "The Taliban are uneducated and ruled by Imams". The livelihood of local families are dependent upon trekkers and mountaineers that will now stay away in droves from the Karakoram as a result of the actions of very few. The Balti people are indeed peaceful, gentle and warm. In that respect they were much like the Iranians. During the midst of things when hope remained alive, I emailed Ramin to let him know that he was in the thoughts and prayers of many in my world. I told him that we all prayed for a miracle. From Islamabad later he replied, "No miracle occurred".

We were driving home from a social gathering a few days after the media had pronounced our three friends dead on the mountain. Commiserating yet again to my girlfriend Joanna about those boys I was sharing little things that I did to tease them and so forth. As we laughed about the small events that filled our bad weather and evacuation days I was struck with the realization that those were really the good days on the mountain. Those were days when we laughed, waited, worried and even sang songs. I remembered the beautiful morning, my best on the mountain, when I was awakened by the singing of Mojtaba in Farsi, his native tongue. He was heralding the arrival of the first rays of sunshine in so many days and echoed our individual sentiments about this break in the weather. I was reminded of a rooster on his perch; how I wished to know the words of his song. His voice was loud and sure as I poked my head from the tent to identify the cause of this vocal eruption. I will forever remember the smile on his face as he raised his arms towards Heaven to thank God for the gift of the promise of that day. I believe that Broad Peak cherry picked the most beautiful fruit of our team and gently folded them under her flanks.

Joanna described what she felt was the peace of their final resting place atop Broad Peak and it's definitely worth sharing,

> *I can see the wind up there. I can see it racing through the thin air making their coats full with ripples. The only sound is the gentle, steady snapping of that crisp fabric. And the only movement is the wind. Cold. Pure. Accentuating their sleepy stillness where they lie surrounded by the snowy blanket of comfort, love, and peace.*
>
> *I think - someday there will be prayer flags at the place where they're resting, - don't you think? So I'm glad to hear that the Iranian flag has been found there already. If they had to die that young, then at least they died doing the very thing they loved more than anything else. I think there's a lot of peace and beauty in that.*

A friend of the Iranians, Helen Chaman, reached out to our team mate Scott Powrie. He shared the following email exchange. It is her unedited translation from Farsi:

Scott

> Ramin & Afshin came back home and they bring stuffs of Aidin, Pouya and Mojtaba, Aidin used to write a diary when he was in there, He mentioned you in his diary. I don't know if anybody has informed you about this, anyway this is the part he mentioned you:
>
> *"As always we have courage to reach base camp, but this year was something different and that was because of our team mates,*
> *There were three Americans, one Canadian, on Mongolian and one Iranian. With us it was 11 people in ATP team. For me, being with*

Americans was most interesting, it was interesting to know about how is their thinking, disciplines, eatings and learning their slangs!
John, Brayan and Scott were Addiction Withdrawal, pilot and production management, Ron was truck driver and Ganga was mountain climbing guide in Mongolia, as time passed we got mixed and we start to think that we are one team, though our goals were different, we care about each other and we enjoyed talks and laughs with them."

And then he write about his feeling and how he suffered when Brian was in pain,
He wrote "it was disgusting to see him in pain, he was elder brother to me."

Regards
Helen

I can tell you that all four of us were moved indescribably to hear this message from beyond the mountain from Aidin. Each of those boys touched us in many ways. In retrospect it wasn't so strange that I had hugged Aidin. Considering what they were attempting I was bidding a younger brother farewell and beseeching his mountain prudence. Aidin's reaction was just like that of a little brother too. He dropped his head and waved it back and forth while smiling dismissively. *"Yeah, yeah, no problem, no problem"* And that was our last conversation.

Below are some thoughts about the passing of our friends, Aidin, Pouya and Mojtaba. To their families I extend the deepest of condolences. To Mojtaba's fiancé I hope she knows that he loved her deeply. To the people of Iran I say there will never be any better ambassadors. To my family and friends I am sorry for the anxiety and worried days our exploits may have caused. To our team I say thanks and goodbye:

We all realize the danger of our sport and impact of it upon our loved ones. Death is not a surprise to mountaineering. You are surrounded by it constantly on 8000-meter peaks and below. You've never been in love until you've had your heart broken. Similarly with mountains, there is no summit that hasn't been paid for dearly by someone else before you. Climbing is essential to humanity for it brings people to the heart and soul of survival. Our race and being depends upon those who challenge the heights, without it we would never have made it to the moon. In fact, we did make it to the moon before conquering many of these earthly giants. That puts our planet in great perspective for me. The Iranians were proudly representing their country in a time when perceptions needed changing. I suspect that Aidin, Pouya and Mojtaba were very cognizant of this and that contributed to the drive to put up this new route.

May you each rest peacefully in a place shared by all faiths. I was proud to have climbed with you, laughed with you and been a part of your team. In whatever good place we may each hope to find ourselves in the afterlife, I look forward to sharing another base camp.

John

Figure 53: Shrine to the Three Musketeers in Iran. Photo compliments of Mohammad Gharaei

STILL CLAIMING VICTIMS

There was another great loss in our war with Broad Peak and the Karakoram that took a couple of months to be realized. For those of us who returned thoughts of what did and didn't transpire on the mountain were as inescapable as the region itself turned out to be. Many were the times Joanna would catch me staring off at a mountain she couldn't see. As much as I wanted to tell her I was thinking of her or our future, I couldn't lie and she would have known anyway. She said, *"All that drama on the mountain was very stressful for me, I didn't like going through it"*. It seemed like our entire relationship hinged upon Broad Peak in some way, shape or form. I wasn't particularly happy reliving parts of it myself. I stayed in almost daily contact with Brian and news of his leg was not particularly encouraging. There was another surgery in preparation for another surgery. Then there were the constant phone calls of people asking what went down. Add to that all the work that was piled up when I returned and my availability, emotional and otherwise was slim.

I emailed Ramin again, now back in Canada. I told him that I hoped he was doing okay but deep down knew there was no way he could ever be resuming any sense of normality. I thought it was important that he knew we were thinking about him. His reply was darker than one would imagine. Apparently many in Iran were blaming him for the deaths of Aidin, Mojtaba and Pouya. People have a need to make it someone's fault and he was bearing the brunt of misguided remorse. People were suggesting that the boys were too young to lead the summit assault. They insinuated that Ramin somehow didn't properly vet the route, that he lacked sufficient experience to lead an 8000 meter peak. To folks who have never climbed it may seem as if these things must be someone's responsibility but nothing is further from reality. Sir John Hunt had never summited an 8000 meter peak either. I suspect had Hillary and Norgay failed on Everest he would have borne the same arrows.

I don't know what transpired in private conversations between the Iranians but words mean little in battle. We were a team but the fight for a summit is individual. Just like in 2011 when Brian turned back, I marched on to the top of Muztagh Ata and escaped with little consequence other than frostbite. Descending in the dark, alone on the mountain high in the Chinese Pamirs on a crystal clear summer night, God spoke to me and brought me safely back to base camp with a headlamp on its final leg with one remaining crampon and a few sips of water. There was a good chance I could have never returned at all. I wasn't listening to the mountain when everyone else turned back due to high winds and sub- zero temperatures. What I brought down from that peak was a lesson that shadowed me throughout the K3 experience. Aidin was a very stubborn and focused young man. He had a summit monkey on his back and, like me in China, could have abandoned some mountain prudence with proximity to the top. I know that a seasoned high altitude climber couldn't turn me around in 2011 and I was definitely old enough to know better.

What I should have been listening to when I returned was the rhythm of something equally important. As storm clouds darkened the Karakoram day after day it was Joanna who kept the home fires burning, disseminating information, worrying and praying. My first week back I was more distant than the mountain itself. As those days turned into months I withdrew into a cocoon of emotional isolation. I wrapped myself in *"Old Yeller"* to stave off intimacy with anyone. We became close to those boys. Like Ramin said, *"they were our little brothers"*. There is little doubt, had they survived, we could have joined forces for another expedition. It was a conversation we kicked around in spite of the differences between our nations. Neither of us could visit the other but we could meet in the mountains and defy all the politics prohibiting our friendship. Our little brothers walked off in the middle of the night for the summit never to return. I should have not been surprised when Joanna, two months later, followed suit. It was more intimacy that she desired; like fresh water at high camp it was the one thing

I was least able to spare. But I was no less shocked the day she gathered up her belongings and disappeared into the moonlight. There was no way she could ever compete with the hulking, miserable mass that had become the vile mountain of heartbreak we came to know as K3.

The End.

www.temptingthethroneroom.com

28800841R00095

Made in the USA
Charleston, SC
22 April 2014